THE LUDLOW LEGACY

The Descendants of Israel Ludlow
(1765-1804)
Surveyor and Pioneer of the Northwest Territory

Mark Mitchell
2015

The Ludlow Legacy
by Mark Mitchell

ISBN 978-0-615-33647-3

Library of Congress Control Number: 2015955029

This work is dedicated to my wife,
Yolanda Dare Mitchell,
and to our children
Matthew Claiborne Mitchell and Chloe Noelle Mitchell.
Thank you for your love, patience and support.

"To Thee I resign my children.
Choose their changes, and make the path of duty plain before them.
Spare them from the rude storms of life.
Impress upon them the importance of truth, and vouchsafe to them the everlasting
inheritance that fadeth not away.
May we all meet in Thy Kingdom!"

A Prayer, Charlotte Chambers Ludlow Riske, 12th January, 1817

CONTENTS

An Introduction to the Ludlow Family

For the two hundred year period of the nineteenth and twentieth centuries, the Ludlow name was well-known, associated with the founding of southwestern Ohio and northern Kentucky, and linked to the rich history of the Northwest Territory and the Ohio River Valley.

Colonel Israel Ludlow was present at the origin of the city of Cincinnati, and his role as a pioneer and founding father of the region became legendary. The Ohio cities of Hamilton and Dayton also were born of his energy and vision.

Perhaps there are those who would discount any comparison between Col. Ludlow and contemporaries such as Daniel Boone or Simon Kenton. Yet like these men, who are rightfully esteemed in American history, Ludlow also traversed wild forests and meadows previously unexplored by men of European descent and opened new frontiers for settlement. Both Boone and Kenton were fortunate to have lived long lives, and both received some recognition during their lifetime for their contributions to our country's history and heritage.

Alas, for Ludlow, it was not meant to be, as he was taken by death in 1804 at the young age of 38. He was mourned and remembered as a great man who was well respected by his superiors; recognized as a great leader among the early settlers and his peers; and a trusted friend to the Native American people, with whom he dealt fairly and justly.

Undoubtedly, his children and grandchildren, were told of his adventures. Even years after his death, the life and legends of Col. Ludlow were told in stories, poetry and song.[i]

His extensive knowledge of the area, obtained through his travels as a surveyor, allowed him to acquire his choice of valuable lands. Within fifty years, Cincinnati had rapidly grown, becoming America's sixth largest city by 1840, and the sale of those lands provided the basis of his family's wealth.

But beyond any inheritance of wealth or fame, Col. Israel Ludlow and Charlotte, left to their descendants an even more important legacy. They were devoted to their visions for the future, and provided examples for their children of lives well-lived, although at the cost of hardship and great personal sacrifice. They left the comforts of a well-established society to face the dangers and difficulties of an untamed wilderness; sought to improve the conditions of the less fortunate; treated all equally with compassion and respect; and taught their children that education and faith are important in life and society. Neither Israel nor Charlotte were to see the results of their labor. If they had been granted long lives, they would have witnessed Cincinnati's growth into a major center of commerce and trade and watched their children become charitable and influential leaders of society and outspoken advocates for equality and freedom.

Over the following generations, the Ludlow family has continued to serve and lead in various ways, such as through the military and in the realm of politics, religion and industry; as artists and authors; inventors and architects and athletes; lawyers, doctors, teachers, and more.

It is that spirit and desire to serve and lead, which is truly the Ludlow legacy.

The Ancestry of Israel Ludlow

According to family tradition, the immigrant ancestors of Israel Ludlow were from the English county of Wiltshire. Immigrants from that area, surnamed Ludlow, traveled to America and their descendants flourished in the new world, in New York, New England and Virginia.

Instead, however, the family of Col. Israel Ludlow was descended from William Ludlam of Matlock, Derbyshire, England, who immigrated to America around 1650. William settled on Long Island, New York, and his descendants moved westward into New Jersey. Along the way, the surname Ludlam was replaced by Ludlow, and so the family came to be known.[ii]

In the years of Israel Ludlow and his family in Cincinnati, two possible sources may have convinced them that their ancestry was through the Wiltshire Ludlows.

One possible source was close family friend General William Henry Harrison. Harrison was a descendant of the Wiltshire Ludlows and, perhaps, believed he shared a common ancestry with Israel Ludlow.

The second possible source of this assumption was the stage actor and manager Noah Miller Ludlow, who descended from Gabriel Ludlow of the Wiltshire line. Well-acquainted with Israel Ludlow's family, and a genealogist himself, it seems likely that he convinced the Ludlows of the Wiltshire lineage. Though none of his family research had found a link between the two families, the assumption seems to have been made that Israel Ludlow was of Wiltshire family descent. Interestingly, many years later, Noah Miller Ludlow published a genealogical work called "A Genealogical History of the Ludlow Family" in 1884. Unable to connect Israel Ludlow's family, they are not included in the work.[iii]

The Ancestry of Israel Ludlow

6) William Ludlam, immigrated to America ca. 1650
   b. 1605, Matlock, Derbyshire, England
   m. Clemence Fordham
   d. 1665, Southampton, NY

5) Henry Ludlam
   b. 1638 Apr 15, Matlock, Derbyshire, England
   m. Jane Shaw
   d. 1691 Oct 25, Southampton, NY

4) Henry Ludlam II
   b. 1668/69 Jan 08, Southampton, NY
   m. Rachel Halsey
   d. 1737 Sep 17, Jamaica, NY

3) Jeremiah Ludlam/Ludlow, first to use Ludlow surname
   b. ca. 1697
   m. Temperance -----
   d. 1764 Aug 01, New Providence, NJ

2) Cornelius Ludlow
   b. 1728, Long Island, NY
   m1 Catherine Cooper
   m2 Martha Lyon
   m3 Mary Wall
   d. 1812 Apr 27, Long Hill, Morris Co., NJ

He was a member of the Eastern Battalion of New Jersey troops raised on January 13th, 1776. He took part in the battle of Long Island as Major in Gen. Heard's Brigade; served as Lieutenant Colonel of the Eastern Battalion to cover Washington's retreat across New Jersey after the evacuation of New York. He served at Trenton, Princeton and Springfield and was wounded at Germantown, October 4th, 1777.

1) Israel Ludlow (1765-1804)

Israel Ludlow Grave Marker
Spring Grove Cemetery
Section 113 Lot 170

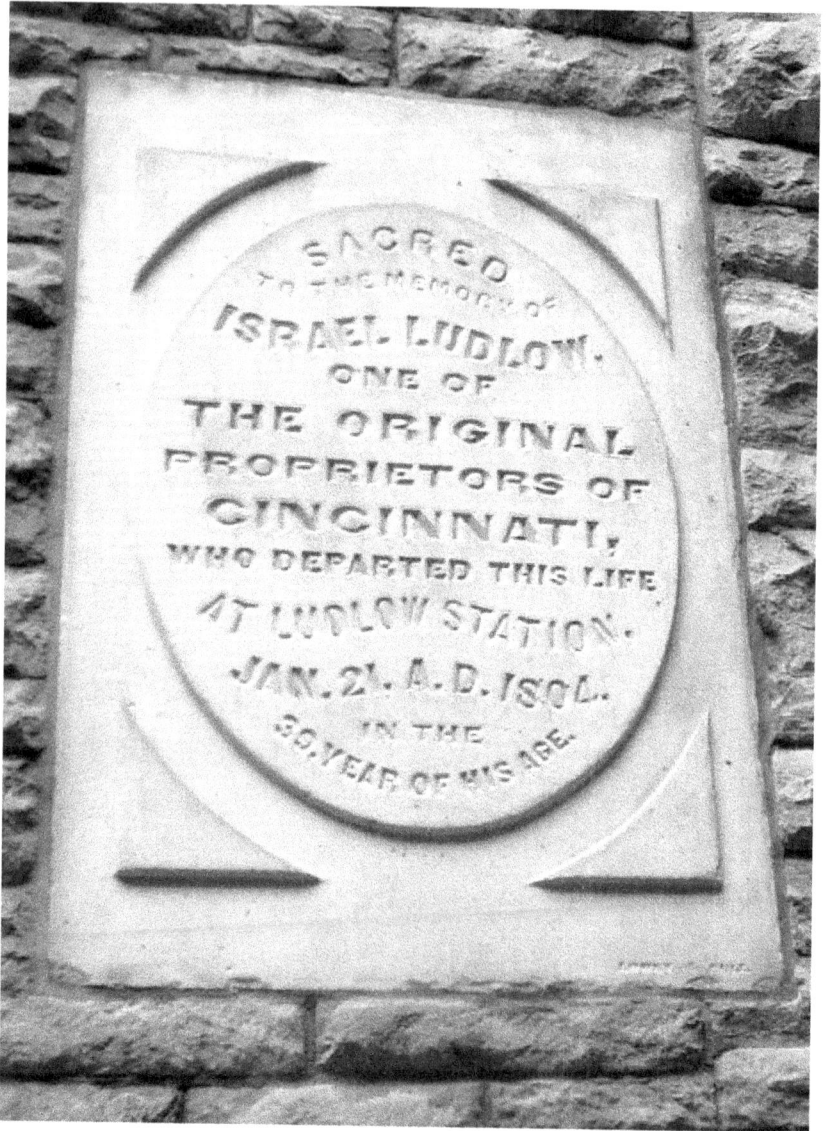

Wall tablet,
"Sacred to the memory of Israel Ludlow"
In the courtyard entryway of Covenant Presbyterian Church,
Cincinnati, Ohio.

Israel Ludlow

1. Israel Ludlow
   b. 1765, Long Hill, Morris Co., NJ
   d. 1804 Jan 21, "Ludlow Station"[iv], OH[v]
   bur: Spring Grove Cemetery, Cincinnati, OH (Section-113 Lot-170)

The son of Cornelius Ludlow and his second wife, Martha Lyon, Israel Ludlow was born at Long Hill, near Morristown, New Jersey.[vi]

At the end of the Revolutionary War, as part of the Treaty of Paris of 1783, the British ceded to the United States a large area of land, north of the Ohio River and west to the Mississippi River, which came to be known as the Northwest Territory. In preparation for the sale of land in the region, it became necessary for the United States government to send surveyors into the area.

It was then in 1787 that Israel Ludlow of New Jersey was contacted and appointed by Thomas Hutchins, Geographer General of the United States, to assist in the survey work in the Northwest Territory.

Ludlow performed surveying services in the Seven Ranges area of eastern Ohio, followed by surveys along the Ohio River. Hutchins then ordered Ludlow to report to Judge John Cleve Symmes to survey the land known as the Symmes Purchase, located between the Great Miami and Little Miami Rivers.

While at the town of Limestone,[vii] Kentucky, Ludlow encountered Matthias Denman, also of New Jersey, who had purchased 800 acres of land from Symmes, and along with partner Robert Patterson of Lexington, proposed to create a settlement on the property. Ludlow was offered to become a third partner in the venture, his role being to survey the new town, and he accepted.

On December 28th, 1788, a group of men landed at a small cove on the north bank of the Ohio River, opposite the mouth of the Licking River, and founded the settlement which later became the city of Cincinnati. The young surveyor quickly proceeded to measure out the lots and streets and by winter's end, Ludlow had platted the town. Although neither Denman nor Patterson remained in Cincinnati, Israel Ludlow made Cincinnati his home.

Ludlow traveled back to New Jersey and encouraged others there to join him in this new land of promise. He was successful, and many of his relatives and friends joined him in Ohio.[viii]

Those early settlers faced many great hardships, but dealing with repeated Indian attacks in the area was their greatest challenge. To provide security to the area, a military outpost, Fort Washington, was established at Cincinnati. The fort was used as the base of operations for army maneuvers against the Indians, and several outposts, called stations, were created in locations surrounding the city.

One of these outposts was built five miles north of Cincinnati by Israel Ludlow on land he owned there, and it became known as Ludlow Station.

For his role in the militia, he became known as Colonel Ludlow.

Other properties Israel Ludlow owned included "large tracts of lands along the Miami and Mad Rivers"[ix], and also along the Mill Creek north of the Ohio River. In October of 1794, "General Jonathan Dayton had acquired the entire third or Military Range of the Miami Purchase. On December 12, 1794, in a fractional section, Ludlow laid out and platted a new town. On July 27, 1795, Ludlow had acquired full ownership of the fractional section of Number 2 in Township 1 and Range III....

Initially, this new town was to be called Fairfield. However, its name was later changed to Hamilton, after Alexander Hamilton. Ludlow became the sole proprietor of that town. He donated a square for public buildings and another square for a church and a cemetery. He also donated $4,200 for the construction of the county court house."[x]

On August 3rd, 1795, a treaty between General Anthony Wayne and several Indian tribes was signed at Fort Greenville. The treaty required the creation of a boundary line, and Ludlow was then hired to perform the survey. This is known as the Greenville Treaty Line.

In November, "Ludlow laid out a new town at the junction of the Great Miami and the Mad Rivers and named it Dayton, after General Jonathan Dayton."[xi]

In the spring of 1796, Ludlow traveled east to New Jersey, and along the way visited with General James Chambers of Chambersburg, and his daughter, Charlotte. Israel and Charlotte were betrothed, and upon Israel's return to Cincinnati, he built a frame house along the banks of the Mill Creek, at Ludlow Station, in preparation for their marriage. This home was referred to as the "Ludlow Mansion", being at that time the largest house in the vicinity.

In the fall of that year, Col. Ludlow, accompanied by associates Benjamin Van Cleve and W. C. Schenck, set out "to survey the United States military lands between the Scioto and Muskingum Rivers". There was a "deep snow...covered in crust...and could kill but little game, and were twenty-nine days without bread and nearly all that time without salt, and sometimes very little to eat. We were five days seven in company, on four meals, and they, except the last, scanty. They consisted of a turkey, two young raccoons, and the last day some rabbits and venison, which we got from some Indians."[xii]

By November 10th, 1796, Ludlow had returned to Chambersburg, and he and Charlotte were married. Ten days afterward, the couple left for Cincinnati through rugged terrain and bitter winter weather.

They did not arrive until February of 1797.

The couple lived in Cincinnati through that summer as the building of the Ludlow Mansion continued, but by the end of the year they had moved into their new home, along with their first born, a son, James Chambers Ludlow.

Continuing his survey work, Colonel Ludlow was often absent from home for long periods of time, leaving Charlotte behind at Ludlow Station to tend the farm and raise their children.

More children were born to them, Martha Catherine Ludlow was born in 1799; and Sarah Bella Ludlow in 1802. In January of 1804, they were preparing for the birth of their fourth child, when Israel Ludlow suddenly took ill and died. In a letter, dated February 3, 1804, Charlotte wrote the following words to her mother...

"How shall I begin my mournful communication? Your heart will sympathize but too tenderly and deeply in my afflictions, deprived as I am of the most amiable, affectionate and indulgent of husbands. I am left alone and stricken to the earth! My children are too young to know their loss, and therefore excite the greater pity. My situation demands the exercise of all my reason and religion.

The Lord gave, and He hath taken away. May I be enabled to say, "Blessed be His name." I know the Judge of all the earth doeth right, whether we can comprehend it or not. This thought, I trust, will sustain me, whatever the bitterness of my portion....

I know that my husband loved and feared the Lord. His heart was governed by the purest Christian principles; and without ostentation or display, his delight was in doing good. The poor will lament his loss, for he was their friend. Not yet recovered from the stunning blow, I find myself inquiring, is it real? Oh, my God, my merciful Father in Heaven, I thank Thee that I have the comforting hope of meeting him again at Thy right hand, no longer in sorrow and tears!...

On Tuesday morning, Mr. Ludlow arose in his usual health, and on Saturday he left me for eternity. Oh, he is dead, my mother! He is gone from me forever! Language is inadequate to express the agony of such a moment!"

Another letter written in that February, from Cincinnatian Elnathan Kemper to his relative William Kemper, stated...

"Colonel Ludlow passed his great and important change on the twenty first of last month, after four days confinement with an inflamatory [sic] fever, he was buried in Cincinnati, followed by a very great prosesion [sic] to the grave. His death will cause a very great over turning of things in this Country....

We could not have lost a man on this side of the mountains whose loss would have been felt anything like his, in the first place to the United States, they have lost the most capable man they have or can get to do their business in this Country, in the second place to society here and in the third place his loss to his family will ever be unknown."[xiii]

A town square in Cincinnati, bounded by Walnut, Main, Fourth and Fifth Streets, was the location of Cincinnati's First Presbyterian Church. It was here that Israel Ludlow's remains were originally laid to rest in the church graveyard. He was buried with full Masonic honors and his eulogy was given by Judge John Cleves Symmes.

His remains were removed to Spring Grove Cemetery in 1896.

m. Charlotte Chambers, 1796 Nov 10, Loudon Forge, PA
b. 1768 Nov 13, Chambersburg, PA
d. 1821 May 20, Franklin, MO
bur: Franklin, MO

The daughter of Gen. James Chambers and Catharine (Hamilton) Chambers, Charlotte was raised in the town of Chambersburg in south-central Pennsylvania. The area had attracted settlers of Scots-Irish descent, which included the Chambers family, and a town was established and named for its founder, her grandfather, Benjamin Chambers.

Charlotte spent part of the winter of 1795 in Philadelphia, at that time the capital of the United States, and enjoyed mingling with the society of that city. While there, she was also a guest of President and Mrs. George Washington. In the spring of 1796, she was introduced to Israel Ludlow and by year's end, they were married and traveling to a new home in Ohio.

While en route to Cincinnati, Charlotte wrote to her mother...

" I assure you, my dear mother, the happiness I had anticipated in wedded life has been more than realized. I was so fearful of the bitterness of disappointment consequent on anticipating too much perfection in the human character, that I approached the subject with subdued and moderate calculations; but my husband's generous affection and admirable character have secured my gratitude and love."[xiv]

"When I arrived, in Feb. 1797,Cincinnati was a village of wooden buildings, with a garrison of soldiers. The society consisted of a small number of ladies, united by the most perfect good-will and desire for mutual happiness. The gentlemen were social and intelligent...."

The couple moved to their home at Ludlow Station, on the Mill Creek, five miles north of Cincinnati, in 1797. Many notable men of the time visited there.

"Emigrating early to the west, I formed an acquaintance with many Indians, several of whom I respected as men of understanding; and I have often heard them lament the distressing situation and the ungovernable passions of their people, and the avarice of the white men."

About the year 1800, in the month of June, Charlotte, who was called "La-nah-pa-kwa" by the Delaware Indians, was visited by two members of the tribe, chief Bok-on-ja-ha-lus and his friend Kin-ka-box-kie. They had been met by Israel in Cincinnati, and instructed by him to stop at Ludlow Station for dinner. "While we sat conversing at the table after the cloth was removed, he [Bok-on-ja-ha-lus] said, "La-nah-pa-kwa, we now go," "And when shall I see you again?" said I. "Me old; me soon lay down," said he, with a horizontal motion of his hand. Then raising his eyes to Heaven, with an ardent emotion, he added with an effusion of feeling I have never seen more expressive, "But we shall meet with Jesus." I took his hand , inquiring with rapture, "Bok-on-ja-ha-lus, do you know Jesus?" He answered with firmness, "Me know Jesus; me love Jesus." Then rising from the table , they shook hands with me, *solemnly saying farewell. My eyes followed their venerable figures until the door closed from my view for the last time in this world Bok-on-ja-ha-lus and his friend."*

At the death of her husband in January of 1804, the young widow and her children left Ludlow Station and moved to Cincinnati, where her fourth child, son Israel L. Ludlow, was born that May.[xv] Charlotte's father died the following year and her mother left Chambersburg for Cincinnati to live with Charlotte. Charlotte married a second time in December of 1808, and she and her family returned to reside at the Ludlow Mansion. [xvi]

Her husband, Rev. David Riske, was an Irish-born minister of the Presbyterian church and with this marriage, she became the devoted wife of a clergyman. The Riske's had two daughters, Ruhamah and Charlotte.

Charlotte became an active member of the American Bible Society, one of the first women to do so, and organized a local chapter of the organization. A letter, addressed to Elias Boudinot, President of the American Bible Society, retold of the encounter with Bok-on-ja-ha-lus years earlier and ended with the following sentence…*"And now, my dear sir, that my faith may not be dead without works, I commit unto your hands , as the friend of humanity, one hundred dollars for the department particularly of the Delaware Translation. With sentiments of respect, I am, dear sir, La-nah-pa-kwa"*

Charlotte, seeing also the "sad conditions of the colored people", organized the creation of "Sabbath schools" and through this the African Association of Cincinnati was formed.

Rev. Riske died in October of 1818, and her mother, Catherine Chambers, died in January of 1820, leaving Charlotte alone to raise her young children.

An illness struck soon afterward and Charlotte, severely weakened, was advised by her doctors that a change in climate may be beneficial. Accompanied by her three youngest children, a woman servant, and a carriage driver, the group left Cincinnati for Missouri, in September of 1820. The first night of their journey was spent at the home of Gen. William Henry Harrison at North Bend, who was there himself to greet them. Travelling westward through the villages of Madison and Vincennes, they eventually crossed the Mississippi River. Arriving at their destination, the journey had been "of nearly six hundred miles, performed in eighteen days".[xvii]

Despite her weakened condition, Charlotte hoped to return with her family to Cincinnati in the spring. Instead, on May 20th, 1821, Charlotte passed away and was buried at Franklin.

Children:

2.0001	i.	+	James Chambers Ludlow
3.0001	ii.	+	Martha Catharine Ludlow
4.0001	iii.	+	Sarah Bella Ludlow
5.0001	iv.	+	Israel L. Ludlow

Ludlow Station
"Near this spot stood the block house at Ludlow Station built in 1791.
General Arthur St. Clair and his army encamped here from Aug. 1st to Sept. 17th 1791.
General Anthony Wayne and his army encamped here in 1793.
Erected by the Cincinnati Chapter Daughters of the American Revolution 1916."

The Ludlow Mansion, 1796-1891

OF HISTORIC FAME

THE OLD LUDLOW MANSION TO BE DEMOLISHED

A Place Where Men of National Reputation Have Congregated.

"The old Israel Ludlow mansion in Cumminsville, and one of, if not the oldest building in Hamilton County, will soon be a thing of the past. It is located on the block of ground bounded by Mad Anthony and Chambers streets on the east and west and Chase Ave and the C., H. and D. Railroad track on the north and south, and contains nearly two acres of ground...

The demolition of this old structure of historic fame, covering as it does a part of two centuries, is deserving of more than a passing notice....

In and out of the portals of the old building have passed General Arthur St. Clair, Colonel Israel Ludlow, John Cleves Symmes, Jared Mansfield, General Anthony Wayne, Governor R. J. Meigs, "Little Turtle" and "Bok-on-ja-ha-lus", the Indian warriors. Ex-President William Henry Harrison, "Tippecanoe"; Governor E. A. Brown, Hon. Lewis Cass, Governor Thomas Worthington, Chief Justice Salmon P. Chase, General J. C. Totten, Judge Burnet, Judge D. K. Este, Judge Goforth, Nicholas Longworth, Hon. Oliver M. Spencer, General Gano, General William Lytle and General J. H. Piatt."

The Cincinnati Enquirer, November 26th, 1891

James Chambers Ludlow Grave Marker

Spring Grove Cemetery
Section 23 Lot 43

James Chambers Ludlow

2.0001 James Chambers 2 Ludlow *(Israel1)*
    b. 1797 Sep 10, Cincinnati, OH
    d. 1841 Aug 15, "Ludlow Station"[xviii], OH[xix]
    bur: Spring Grove Cemetery, Cincinnati, OH (Section-23 Lot-43)

Named for his maternal grandfather, James Chambers Ludlow, was born at
Ludlow Station in 1797. At the age of 6, his father died, and his mother and
siblings moved to Cincinnati. "Although reared amidst the wilderness and
dangers of pioneer life, he received a superior education, and became the
beneficent genius of his neighborhood. He inherited a large estate and
devoted much time and money to philanthropic work."[xx] In 1817, James left
Cincinnati and relocated at Franklin, Missouri, where he sought to build his
future as a miller and merchant. He returned to Cincinnati in 1819 to marry
Josephine Dunlop, and she accompanied him back to Missouri. His mother,
Charlotte, and his youngest siblings joined him at Franklin in the autumn of
1820. During the winter months, Charlotte's health declined and James
prepared to return with the family to Cincinnati. He advertised for sale his mill
and mercantile business, but the building and its contents burned to the
ground in the spring of 1821. Shortly afterward, Charlotte passed away and
James brought the family back to Ludlow Station.
There arrived in Cincinnati, in 1822, cousins from the Chambers side of the
family, who had left Maryland to find a new home at Cincinnati. The Cloppers,
headed by patriarch Nicholas Clopper, were interested in acquiring land in
Texas, but in the meantime, they settled into a home at Ludlow Station given to
them by James Ludlow, which they called Beechwood.
In 1826, James, Israel and Nicholas Clopper sailed south to Matagorda Bay,
Texas. Among their traveling companions was David G. Burnet. This was a
return trip for Burnet who had suffered from consumption, gone to Texas and
had "gradually recovered health by living an outdoor life with the Indians".[xxi]
Upon their arrival, Nicholas Clopper and the Ludlow brothers found the area
desirable as a place of residence. They returned to Cincinnati, but never forgot
their favorable impression of the area, nor the account of David Burnet's
miraculous recovery.
In 1832, in the "interest of education, literature and religion", James built a
house called the "Hall of Free Discussion", as a result of Cincinnati's Lane
Theological Seminary banning the debate over the slavery issue. This became a
meeting hall to discuss the subject of slavery and other controversial topics of
the day. Here, abolitionist speakers such as Rev. Lyman Beecher, Theodore

Weld and William Cary addressed the issue of slavery. Black students were even taught in this building in preparation for attending Ohio's Oberlin College. In April of 1835, the Ohio Anti-Slavery Society was founded. The organization sent lecturers throughout the state to encourage the abolition of slavery. Their message was also spread through a newspaper, "The Philanthropist". By the end of 1836, their membership numbered ten thousand. At the first annual meeting, members decided that an Executive Committee based in Cincinnati should govern the society."[xxii] James was named the president of the organization. Also important leaders in the Cincinnati society included James G. Birney, publisher of "The Philanthropist" and Gamaliel Bailey, the paper's editor. Many Cincinnati businesses depended on southern trade, so when "The Philanthropist" was published, business leaders rioted and destroyed the printing press. Undaunted, the press was replaced, the newspapers were printed and the mobs returned to continue the destruction. The mobs were expected at Ludlow Station, too, but never appeared. The society, and its newspaper, continued their work, and James Ludlow remained as its president until 1840.

On August 15, 1841, due to consumption, James Chambers Ludlow passed away at his home at Ludlow Station.

On the first anniversary of his death his cousin, Rebecca Clopper wrote these lines in tribute to him:

"In thee the virtues all did blend:
Thou ever wert the stranger's friend.
The poor thou succour'd in distress,
The widow and the fatherless---
To all would ever lend thine aid,
And thus thy virtues were display'd." [xxiii]

m. Josephine Dunlop, 1819 Mar 30, Cincinnati, OH
b. 1799, Chambersburg, PA
d. 1845 Dec 07, "Ludlow Station", OH[xxiv]
bur: Spring Grove Cemetery, Cincinnati, OH (Section-23 Lot-42)

Children:

2.1001	i.	+	Sarah Bella Dunlop Ludlow	
2.1002	ii.	+	James Dunlop Ludlow	
2.1003	iii.	+	Charlotte Chambers Ludlow	
2.1004	iv.	+	Catherine Ludlow	
2.1005	v.	+	Benjamin Chambers Ludlow	
2.1006	vi.	+	Ruhamah Ludlow	
2.1007	vii.	+	Josephine Ludlow	(1837-1866)
2.1008	viii.	+	Israel Ludlow	

2.1001 Sarah Bella Dunlop "Belle"₃ Ludlow *(James 2 Israel 1)*

    b. 1820 Apr 20, "Ludlow Station", OH
    d. 1852 Jan 13, Cincinnati, OH[xxv]
    bur: Spring Grove Cemetery, Cincinnati, OH (Section-30 Lot-11)

    m. Salmon Portland Chase, 1846 Nov 6
    b. 1808 Jan 13, Cornish, NH
    d. 1873 May 07, New York, NY
    bur: Spring Grove Cemetery, Cincinnati, OH (Section-30 Lot-11)

    Son of Ithamar Chase and Janet (Ralston) Chase. Attended Dartmouth College, graduating in 1826. Moved west to Cincinnati, Ohio, in 1830, where he became a prominent lawyer. During the trials and legal proceedings involving James Ludlow, James Birney, and Gamaliel Bailey and the publication of the anti-slavery newspaper, "The Philanthropist", Chase stepped in as counsel to represent them in court. By his marriage to James Ludlow's daughter, Chase became a member of the Ludlow family, and remained a close family ally for the remainder of his life.

Chase was an outspoken abolitionist and a member of the Cincinnati chapter of the Anti-Slavery Society. Entering the political arena, Chase served as Ohio Senator to the US Congress, 1849-1855 and as Governor of Ohio, 1856-1860. Although he sought the 1860 Republican party nomination for president, Abraham Lincoln was selected, and won the presidency. Lincoln then appointed Chase as his Secretary of the United States Treasury. During his administration, The Bureau of Internal Revenue, later known as the Internal Revenue Service, was created in 1862. Chase was credited with placing the motto "In God We Trust" on American currency, and his image was placed on the $10,000 bill. Despite Lincoln's bid for re-election, Chase pursued the presidency in advance of the 1864 presidential election, but his political ambitions were exposed and he resigned from his cabinet position. Months later, President Lincoln nominated Chase as Chief Justice of the US Supreme Court, a position he filled until his death in 1873. Among his achievements as Chief Justice, Chase appointed the first African-American attorney to argue cases before the Supreme Court. Chase also administered the oath of office to President Lincoln for his second term and presided over the impeachment trial of President Andrew Johnson in 1868.

Chase died in New York City and was originally buried at Oak Hill Cemetery in Washington, DC. His remains were later reinterred in Cincinnati's Spring Grove Cemetery in 1886.[xxvi]

Children:

2.2001 i.	+ Janet Ralston Chase	
2.2002 ii.	Josephine Ludlow Chase	(1849-1850)

2.2001 Janet Ralston "Nettie" 4 Chase *(SarahBella3 James2 Israel1)*
        b. 1847 Sep 19, Cincinnati, OH
        d. 1925 Nov 19, Thomasville, GA[xxvii]
        bur: Laurel Hill Cemetery, Thomasville, GA

A noted artist, she founded a decorative arts school in Pelham, New York. She spent her final years at "Pinerift", her cottage in Thomasville, Georgia.[xxviii]

        m. William Sprague Hoyt, 1871 Mar 23, Washington, DC
        b. 1847 Jan 01, New York, NY
        d. 1905 Apr 27, San Juan, PR[xxix]
        bur: Woodland Cemetery, Stamford, CT (Section-G Lot-70)

        Son of Edwin Hoyt and Susan (Sprague) Hoyt. He was a partner in Hoyt, Sprague & Co., a dry goods mercantile business owned by his father. The business suffered bankruptcy in 1873.

Children:

2.3001 i.   Janet Ralston Hoyt   (1872-1947)
2.3002 ii. + Edwin Chase Hoyt
2.3003 iii. + Franklin Chase Hoyt
2.3004 iv. + Beatrix Hoyt

2.3002 Edwin Chase "Winnie" 5 Hoyt *(Janet4 SarahBella3 James2 Israel1)*
        b. 1873 Mar 05, Astoria, NY
        d. 1956 Oct 21, Brentwood, NY[xxx]
        bur: Woodland Cemetery, Stamford, CT (Section-G Lot-70)

Corporate lawyer of New York City.

        m. Maria Louisa "Molly" Moran, 1910 Apr 27, Long Island, NY[xxxi]
        b. 1881 Feb 26, New York, NY
        d. 1965 Aug 06, New York, NY[xxxii]
        bur: Woodland Cemetery, Stamford, CT (Section-G Lot-70)

Children:

2.4001 i. + Nancy Hoyt
2.4002 ii. + Barbara Chase Hoyt
2.4003 iii. + Rosalie Chase Hoyt
2.4004 iv. + Edwin Chase Hoyt, Jr.

2.4001 Nancy 6 Hoyt *(Edwin5 Janet4 SarahBella3 James2 Israel1)*
> b. 1911 May 23, Commack, NY
> d. 1987 Oct 26, Bath, ME
> bur: c
>
> m. George Clair "Jim" St. John Jr., 1936 Dec 19, Islip, NY
> b. 1910 Dec 04, New Haven, CT
> d. 1993 Dec 27, Concord, MA
> bur: c

Son of George Clair St. John and Clara Hitchcock (Seymour) St. John.

Children:

2.5001	i.	+ Clara Seymour St. John
2.5002	ii.	+ Michael St. John
2.5003	iii.	+ Sarah Hoyt St. John
2.5004	iv.	+ Christopher St. John
2.5005	v.	+ Barbara St. John

2.5001 Clara Seymour 7 St. John *(Nancy6 Edwin5 Janet4 SarahBella3 James2 Israel1)*
> b. 1938, CT

She studied music at Harvard under conductor G. Wallace Woodworth and trained at Juilliard for her master's degree. She founded the New Amsterdam Singers, a choral group of New York City, in 1968, and from that time has served as the Musical Director. She has served as the guest conductor for the Juilliard Chorus and Orchestra, the New York Choral Society, and numerous other musical organizations.[xxxiii]

> m. Bevis Longstreth, 1963 Aug 10, Weston, MA
> b. 1934, NY

Son of Bevis Longstreth and Mary Agnes (Shiras) Longstreth. Lawyer and partner in the New York law firm of Debevoise & Plimpton; member, US Securities and Exchange Commission.
Author of "*Spindle and Bow*" and "*Return of the Shade*".[xxxiv]

Children:

2.6001	i.	+ Katherine Shiras Longstreth
2.6002	ii.	+ Thomas Day Longstreth
2.6003	iii.	+ Benjamin Hoyt Longstreth

2.6001 Katherine Shiras 8 Longstreth *(Clara7 Nancy6 Edwin5 Janet4 SarahBella3 James2 Israel1)*
b. 1966, NY

m. David Michael Terry, 1995 Sep 30, Garrison, NY
b. 1965, NY

Son of Harry and Virginia Terry.

Children:

2.7001	i.	Lucas Michael Longstreth Terry	b. 1998
2.7002	ii.	Stella Day Longstreth Terry	b. 2002
2.7003	iii.	Malcolm Courage Longstreth Terry	b. 2002

2.6002 Thomas Day 8 Longstreth *(Clara7 Nancy6 Edwin5 Janet4 SarahBella3 James2 Israel1)*
b. 1967, NY

Head of Resource, a non-profit organization based in Burlington, VT.

m. Julie Elin Mauer, 1997 Oct 04, Phippsburg, ME
b. 1965

Children:

2.7004	i.	Hector Hudson Longstreth	b.2004
2.7005	ii.	Ebbe Sequin Longstreth	b. 2006
2.7006	iii.	Astrid Meridian Longstreth	b. 2009

2.6003 Benjamin Hoyt 8 Longstreth *(Clara7 Nancy6 Edwin5 Janet4 SarahBella3 James2 Israel1)*
b. 1971, NY

Graduate of Williams College and Columbia University Law School. Served as summer intern in the New York State Attorney General's Bureau of the Environment . He clerked for the Chief Judge of the Second Circuit and, at present, works for Natural Resources Defense Council on climate change policy.

m. Molly Elissa Rauch, 2000 Jul 02, Iona Island, NY[xxxv]
b. 1972, NY

Children:

2.7007	i.	Elka Junniper Longstreth	b. 2003
2.7008	ii.	Isaiah Wolf Longstreth	b. 2006
2.7009	iii.	Silas Obadiah Longstreth	b. 2008

2.5002 Michael 7 St. John *(Nancy6 Edwin5 Janet4 SarahBella3 James2 Israel1)*
      b. 1940, CT

      m1 Cornelia Anne Scheffey, 1963 Sep 08, Haverford, PA (div. 1975)
      b. 1940, PA

      m2 Maria Theresa "MT" Alvarez, 1986 Jun 24
      b. 1950, Cuba

Children:

2.6004	i.	Maria Seymour St. John	b. 1965, DC
2.6005	ii.	Benjamin Thun St. John	b. 1966, DC
2.6006	iii.	Nicholas Hoyt St. John	b. 1969, CA
2.6007	iv.	Matthias St. John	b. 1969, CA

2.5003 Sarah Hoyt 7 St. John *(Nancy6 Edwin5 Janet4 SarahBella3 James2 Israel1)*
      b. 1943, CT

      m. Peter Volkert, 1969 Jan 27, Cambridge, MA (div.)
      b. 1939, Indonesia

Children:

2.6008	i.	Ezekiel Volkert	b. 1973
2.6009	ii.	Jannéke Arianne Volkert	b. 1977

2.5004 Christopher "Kit" 7 St. John *(Nancy6 Edwin5 Janet4 SarahBella3 James2 Israel1)*
      b. 1945, CT

Earned B.A. in African History, Harvard College, 1967; M.A. in Area Studies from the London School of African and Oriental Studies, 1968; J.D. from Yale, 1975.

      m1 Maida Elizabeth Solomon, 1970 May 28, Harrison, ME (div.)
      b. 1946, MA

      m2 Eunice Chornish, 1982 Aug 26, Bowdoinham, ME
      b. 1938, NY

Children(m1):

2.6010	i.	Keshia Rebecca Solomon Sanchez	b. 1975, El Salvador

2.5005 Barbara 7 St. John *(Nancy6 Edwin5 Janet4 SarahBella3 James2 Israel1)*
   b. 1949, ME

B.A. in Child Development, Harvard, 1971; B.S. in Biology, Bates College, 1981.

   m. Peter Douglas Vickery, 1970 Jun 20, Phippsburg, ME
   b. 1949, England

   Son of Walter Neef Vickery and Eugenia (Belikoff) Vickery. Earned B.A. in English, Connecticut College, 1972; M.S. in Wildlife Management, University of Maine at Orono, 1990; Ph.D in Wildlife Management, 1992.

Children:

2.6011	i.	Gabriel St. John Vickery	b. 1987, Honduras
2.6012	ii.	Simon Ishmael Vickery	b. 1989, ME

2.4002 Barbara Chase 6 Hoyt *(Edwin5 Janet4 SarahBella3 James2 Israel1)*
   b. 1912 Nov 26, New York, NY
   d. 1965 Nov 01, New York, NY[xxxvi]
   bur: Woodlawn Cemetery, Bronx, NY

Attended Black Mountain College in North Carolina and studied art in Europe and New York. [xxxvii]

   m. Isaac Newton Phelps Stokes, 1940 Feb 24, Thomasville, GA[xxxviii]
   b. 1906 Oct 10, New Haven, CT
   d. 1998 Aug 04, Hanover, NH[xxxix]
   bur: Woodlawn Cemetery, Bronx, NY

   Son of Rev Anson Phelps Stokes and Carol (Mitchell) Stokes. Attended St. Paul's School, Concord, New Hampshire. Graduated from Yale University, 1929; Harvard Law School, 1933. Hired in 1946 by the Department of State, working to secure the choice of Manhattan as the site of that organization's headquarters. President Truman appointed him as chief counsel of the Commerce Department, 1948. He moved to Paris in 1949, serving as general counsel of the Marshall Plan. Returning to New York in 1953, he became a founding partner of the law firm Fleischmann Stokes & Hitchcock. [xl]

Children:

2.5006 i.   +   Samuel Newton Stokes
2.5007 ii. +   Thomas Hoyt Stokes
2.5008 iii. +   Janet Ralston Chase Stokes
2.5009 iv. +   Olivia Phelps Stokes
2.5010 v.   +   Mitchell Phelps Stokes

2.5006 Samuel Newton 7 Stokes *(Barbara 6 Edwin 5 Janet4 Sarah Bella3 James 2 Israel1)*
        b. 1940, NY

Graduated from Yale University in 1963 with a B.A. in History and was a Richard King Mellon fellow at Yale's School of Forestry and Environmental Studies. Served as a Peace Corps Volunteer in Cote d'Ivoire (1963-65) teaching middle school Science and English and Peace Corps Country Director in Benin (1967-70), focusing on agricultural development. He was the Mid-Atlantic Regional Director of the National Trust for Historic Preservation (1976-81) and the Director of the Rivers, Trails, and Conservation Assistance Program for the National Park Service (1991-2006). President of the board of the Marpat Foundation, which supports nonprofit organizations in the Washington, DC, area. He is the principal author of "Saving America's Countryside: A Guide to Rural Conservation" (second edition, 1997, Johns Hopkins University Press). [xli]

        m. Sally Ruth Sims, 1988 Nov 05, Mitchellville MD
        b. 1950, PA

Graduate of the College of William and Mary, Williamsburg, VA; B.A. in Government, 1972; St. Mary's College of Maryland Summer Archaeology Field School (National Endowment for the Humanities Fellow), 1974; The George Washington University, Washington, DC: (National Endowment for the Humanities Fellow), M.A., American Studies, 1975; Clarion University of Pennsylvania (National Endowment for the Humanities Fellow), M.S., Library Science, 1982; founding curator of the National Trust for Historic Preservation Library Collection at the University of Maryland. In 2004 became a White House History Fellow and in 2005 joined the staff of the White House Historical Association, serving as co-curator of the Smithsonian exhibit, "The Working White House". In 2005, began teaching at the Catholic University of America, and currently teaches two courses: History and Theory of Cultural Heritage Institutions, and Art and Museum Librarianship. [xlii]

Children:

2.6013 i.   +   Thomas Wiatt Stokes

2.6013 Thomas Wiatt 8 Stokes (Samuel7 Barbara 6 Edwin 5 Janet4 SarahBella3 James 2 Israel1)
       b. 1990

At Yale University, he was co-founder and designer of the Yale Undergraduate Film Review; Zone leader for the Spring Salvage program of the Yale Office of Sustainability and Custodial Services. Graduated from Yale in 2012 with a B.A. in Fine Arts with a concentration in Film and also earned a certificate in Film from the Fine Arts Academy in Prague. He has held an internship at the National Institutes of Health Institute of Arthritis, Musculoskeletal and Skin Diseases and worked for the Maryland-National Capital Park and Planning Commission in database and online map and graphic design.

2.5007 Thomas Hoyt 7 Stokes *(Barbara 6 Edwin 5 Janet4 Sarah Bella3 James 2 Israel1)*
       b. 1944, DC

       m. Katherine Helene Fletcher, 2008 Apr 19, Stockbridge, MA
       b. 1958

2.5008 Janet Ralston Chase 7 Stokes *(Barbara 6 Edwin 5 Janet4 Sarah Bella3 James 2 Israel1)*
       b. 1946, DC

2.5009 Olivia Phelps 7 Stokes *(Barbara 6 Edwin 5 Janet4 Sarah Bella3 James 2 Israel1)*
       b. 1951, France

"Graduate from Yale University with a B.A. in Psychology; a Master's degree in Social Work from Smith College, and a Master's degree in Public Administration from Harvard University's Kennedy School of Government. Serves as the Executive Director, head of programs, and lead trainer for the Karuna Center for Peacebuilding,"[xliii] a non-profit organization whose mission is "to promote cultures of peace through the transformation of violent conflict".[xliv]

       m. Alexander Dreier, 1976 Mar 20, Forest Row, England
       b. 1948, DC

       Son of John Caspar Dreier and Louisa Cabot (Richardson) Dreier.

Children:

2.6014 i.   + Matthew Brendan Dreier
2.6015 ii. + Lucas Casper Dreier

2.6014 Matthew Brendan 8 Dreier *(Samuel7 Barbara 6 Edwin 5 Janet4 SarahBella3 James2 Israel1)*
b. 1978, Harlemville, NY

m. Helena -----, 2011 Sep 10, Czech Republic

Children:

2.7010 i.   Nicole Elizabeth Dreier

2.6015 Lucas Caspar 8 Dreier *(Samuel7 Barbara 6 Edwin 5 Janet4 SarahBella3 James2 Israel1)*
b. 1980, MA

2.5010 Mitchell Phelps 7 Stokes *(Barbara 6 Edwin 5 Janet4SarahBella3 James2 Israel1)*
b. 1954, NY

m. Maria Cristina Jorge Squeff, 1986 Jun 08, Jericho, VT
b. 1954, Brazil

Children:

2.6016	i.	Barbara Hoyt Squeff Stokes	b. 1987, IL
2.6017	ii.	Daniel Camargo Stokes	b. 1990, NJ

2.4003 Rosalie Chase 6 Hoyt *(Edwin5 Janet4 SarahBella3 James2 Israel1)*
b. 1914 May 20, NY
d. 2006 Jul 25, Brunswick, ME
bur: c

Graduated from the Chapin School, New York City. Professor of Physics at Bryn Mawr College. Served as chair of the Physics department, 1969-1977. In 1969, she was awarded the Lindback Award for Distinguished Teaching.

2.4004 Edwin Chase 6 Hoyt, Jr. *(Edwin5 Janet4 SarahBella3 James2 Israel1)*
b. 1916 Aug 03, Brentwood, NY
d. 2007 Nov 20, Brunswick, ME
bur: Woodland Cemetery, Stamford, CT (Section-G Lot-69)

Professor emeritus of International Law and American Foreign Policy at the University of New Mexico.

m. Mary Hazard, 1953 Apr 02, Peacedale, RI (div.)
b. 1927 Apr 12, Providence, RI
d. 2013 May 13, Oakland, CA
bur: Wacousta Cemetery, Wacousta, MI

Children:

2.5011 i.   +   William Bushnell Hoyt
2.5012 ii. +   Maria Louisa Hoyt
2.5013 iii. +   Emily Elizabeth Hoyt

2.5011 William Bushnell 7 Hoyt *(Edwin6 Edwin5 Janet4 SarahBella3 James2 Israel1)*
      b. 1954, NY

      m. Dru Ellen Wardell, 1981 Nov 06, Mentor, OH
      b. 1954, OH

2.5012 Maria Louisa 7 Hoyt *(Edwin6 Edwin5 Janet4 SarahBella3 James2 Israel1)*
      b. 1956, NY

Graduated cum laude from Connecticut College; received a master's
degree in public administration from New York University.
Author of "Sustaining the League of Women Voters in America". [xlv]

      m. Stephen Douglas Cashin, 1986 Aug 2, Arroyo Seco, NM
      b. 1957, Libya

Son of Richard Marshal Cashin and Mary (Walsh) Cashin. Graduate of
Groton School; Georgetown University. Received his MBA from Boston College.

2.5013 Emily Elizabeth 7 Hoyt *(Edwin6 Edwin5 Janet4 SarahBella3 James2 Israel1)*
      b. 1958, NY

      m. Eric Blossom, 1988

2.3003 Franklin Chase 5 Hoyt *(Janet4 SarahBella3 James2 Israel1)*
      b. 1876 Sep 07, Pelham, NY
      d. 1937 Nov 13, New York, NY [xlvi]
      bur: Wappinger's Rural Cemetery, Wappinger's Falls, NY

      m. Maud Rives Borland, 1918 Jun 08, Wappinger's Falls, NY
      b. 1886 Apr 14, New York, NY
      d. 1982 Apr 07, New York, NY
      bur: Wappinger's Rural Cemetery, Wappinger's Falls, NY

Children:

2.4005 i.   +   Constance Maud Hoyt
2.4006 ii. +   Beatrix Chase Hoyt

2.4005 Constance Maud 6 Hoyt *(Franklin5 Janet4 SarahBella3 James2 Israel1)*

  b. 1919 Mar 25, New York, NY
  d. 1974 Feb 11, Auburn, NY
  bur: Fort Hill Cemetery, Auburn, NY (Section-Hillcrest Lot-48A)

  m. David McDonald Moore, 1943 May 15, New York, NY
  b. 1918 Jan 30, Auburn, NY
  d. 1988 Jan 20, Auburn, NY
  bur: Fort Hill Cemetery, Auburn, NY (Section-Hillcrest Lot-48A)

  Son of Rev. Frank W. Moore and Margaret Stevens (Otheman).

Children:

2.5014 i.   + Franklin Hoyt Moore
2.5015 ii.   + Margaret Moore
2.5016 iii. + Rosamund Beatrix Moore

2.5014 Franklin Hoyt 7 Moore *(Constance6 Franklin5 Janet4 SarahBella3 James2 Israel1)*

  b. 1946, NY

  m1 Carol Hughes Stanco, 1969 Apr 19, New York, NY (div.1977)
  b. 1946, NY

  m2 Robert Hale Bancroft Winsor, Jr., 2004 Sep 11, Nantucket, MA
  b. 1955

Children(m1):

2.6018 i.   Margaret Otheman Moore   b. 1971, NJ
2.6019 ii.   + Natalie Hancock Moore

2.6019 Natalie Hancock 8 Moore *(Franklin7 Constance6 Franklin5 Janet4 SarahBella3 James2 Israel1)*

  b. 1974, NJ

  m. Patrick Louis Clavette, 2000 Oct 07, Hartford, CT
  b. 1969

Children:

2.7011 i.   Eleanor Hancock Clavette   b. 2003, CT
2.7012 ii.   Timothy Moore Clavette   b. 2008, CT

2.5015 Margaret "Peg" 7 Moore *(Constance6 Franklin5 Janet4 SarahBella3 James2 Israel1)*
  b. 1948 Nov 22, Auburn, NY
  d. 2014 Jun24, Auburn, NY
  bur: Fort Hill Cemetery, Auburn, NY (Section-Hillcrest Lot-48A)

  (=) Ralph Main,
  m Joseph Feneck, 1978 Jun 24 (div.1985)

Children(=):

2.6020 i.   +   Shaunna Lee Main

2.6020 Shaunna Lee 8 Main *(Margaret7 Constance6 Franklin5 Janet4 SarahBella3 James2 Israel1)*
  b. 1970, NY

    m1 Gregory Van Epps, 1994 Jul 02, Auburn, NY (div.)
    m2 Robert Eugene Anderson, Jr., 2010 Nov 20, Union Springs, NY

Children(m1):

2.7013 i.	Ashley Margaret Van Epps	(1996)
2.7014 ii.	Connor David Van Epps	b. 1999, NY
2.7015 iii.	McKenzie Margaret-Ann Van Epps	b. 2001, NY

Children(m2):

2.7016 i.	Spencer Edwin Eugene Anderson	b. 2012, NY

2.5016 Rosamund Beatrix "Roz" 7 Moore *(Constance6 Franklin5 Janet4 SarahBella3 James2 Israel1)*
  b. 1949, NY

    m. Paul Austin Lovenduski, 1994 Oct 09, Auburn, NY

2.4006 Beatrix Chase "Trixie" 6 Hoyt *(Franklin5 Janet4 SarahBella3 James2 Israel1)*
    b. 1920 Jul 09, New York, NY
    d. 2005 Nov 10, Oyster Bay, NY[xlvii]
    bur: Wappinger's Rural Cemetery, Wappinger's Falls, NY

    m1 Park Benjamin Jr., 1940 Sep 21, Wappinger's Falls, NY
    b. 1917 Mar 18, New York, NY
    d. 1986 Sep 08, Oyster Bay, NY
    bur: Wappinger's Rural Cemetery, Wappinger's Falls, NY

    Son of Park Benjamin Sr. and Katharine Ward (Doremus) Benjamin.

m2 Stephen Howland Taylor, 1987 Oct 19
b. 1931, Fall River, MA
d. 2007 Apr 28, Oyster Bay, NY
bur: Wappinger's Rural Cemetery, Wappinger's Falls, NY

Children(m1):

2.5017 i.   + Park Benjamin III
2.5018 ii. + Hoyt Doremus Benjamin
2.5019 iii. + William Chase Benjamin
2.5020 iv. + Stephen Delancey Benjamin

2.5017 Park 7 Benjamin III *(Beatrix6 Franklin5 Janet4 Sarah Bella3 James2 Israel1)*

  b. 1943, NY

  m. Candice Lee Jennings, 1969, NY

Children:

2.6021 i.   + Park Benjamin IV
2.6022 ii. + John Jennings Benjamin

2.6021 Park 8 Benjamin IV *(Park7 Beatrix6 Franklin5 Janet4 Sarah Bella3 James2 Israel1)*

  b. 1971, NY

  m. Amanda Carroll

Children:

2.7017	i.	Avery Elizabeth Benjamin	b. 2005, NJ
2.7018	ii.	Caroline Paige Benjamin	b. 2008, NJ

2.6022 John Jennings 8 Benjamin *(Park7 Beatrix6 Franklin5 Janet4 Sarah Bella3 James2 Israel1)*

  b. 1974, NY

Graduate of Boston University; Senior Art Director in the Auckland, New Zealand office the advertising agency, Saatchi & Saatchi.

  m. Kirsten Isaksen, 2005 Sep 17, Oyster Bay, NY[xlviii]

Children:

2.7019	i.	Sophie Cyr Benjamin	b. 2007, NY
2.7020	ii.	Isobel Chase Benjamin	b. 2012, NY

2.5018 Hoyt Doremus 7 Benjamin *(Beatrix6 Franklin5 Janet4 SarahBella3 James2 Israel1)*
b. 1945, NY

m. Rebecca Smith, 1988, NY

Children:

2.6023 i.	Hoyt Doremus Benjamin Jr.	b. 1988, NY
2.6024 ii.	Chase Rives Benjamin	b. 1991, NY

2.5019 William Chase 7 Benjamin *(Beatrix6 Franklin5 Janet4 SarahBella3 James2 Israel1)*
b. 1947, NY

m. Karen Kay Horton, 1974, VT
b. 1946, OH

Children:

2.6025 i.	Sarah Lloyd Benjamin	b. 1976, Belgium
2.6026 ii.	Lisa Katherine Benjamin	b. 1978, CT
2.6027 iii.	Alexandra Chase Benjamin	b. 1982, NY

2.5020 Stephen Delancey 7 Benjamin *(Beatrix6 Franklin5 Janet4 SarahBella3 James2 Israel1)*
b. 1955, NY

Earned his B.A. degree from Yale University; has extensive sailing experience as National College Sailor of the Year (1978, Yale); 3-Time World Champion-Fireball (1976 & 1977), 505 (1980); U.S. Olympic Silver Medalist in the 470 Class as helm (1984); 5 Admiral's Cups-1st in Class in BRAVURA (1991);Yale Sailing Associate Chairman (1993-2013); Sailing Yacht Research Foundation (SYRF) Chairman; Hudson River Community Sailing (HRCS) Board of Directors; Board of Directors, United States Sailing.[xlix]

m. Helen "Heidi" Ziegler, 1992 Jul 11
b. 1961

2.3004 Beatrix 5 Hoyt *(Janet4 SarahBella3 James2 Israel1)*
b. 1880 Jul 05, Wappinger's Falls, NY
d. 1963 Aug 14, Thomasville, GA
bur: Laurel Hill Cemetery, Thomasville, GA

At age 16, she became the youngest golfer to win the U. S. Women's Amateur, a record that stood until 1971. After retiring from golf, she became an artist, concentrating on sculpture and landscape painting.[l]

2.1002 James Dunlop "Dun"3 Ludlow *(James 2 Israel 1)*
> b. 1822 Oct 30, "Ludlow Station", OH
> d. 1886 Oct 09, Paxton, IL
> bur: Glen Cemetery, Paxton, IL (Section-7 Lot-5)

"He was highly respected by his neighbors and friends for his excellent character and sterling worth. He was for many years a resident of Ludlow, Champaign County, which is named in his honor."[li]

> m. Susan Middlecoff, 1862 May 20
> b. 1839 Oct 22, Wayne Co. IN
> d. 1897 Dec 04, Paxton, IL
> bur: Glen Cemetery, Paxton, IL (Section-7 Lot-5)

Children:

2.2004	i.	+ Samuel F. Ludlow	
2.2005	ii.	Sarah Bella Ludlow	(1865-1867)
2.2006	iii.	+ Theresa Ludlow	
2.2007	iv.	+ Edmund Ludlow	
2.2008	v.	Charlotte Ludlow	(1871-1872)
2.2009	vi.	+ Katharine Ludlow	
2.2010	vii.	Clara D. Ludlow	(1879-1880)

2.2004 Samuel F. 4 Ludlow *(James 3 James 2 Israel 1)*
> b. 1863 Apr 27, Ludlow, IL
> d. 1949 Sep 02, Paxton, IL[lii]
> bur: Glen Cemetery, Paxton, IL (Section-7 Lot-5)

Practiced law in Paxton, Illinois, for fifty years. Served two terms as city attorney, two terms as mayor and two terms as county judge.

> m. Della Martin, 1890 Oct 10, Paxton, IL
> b. 1870 Aug 07, Gifford, IL
> d. 1938 Apr 19, Paxton, IL
> bur: Glen Cemetery, Paxton, IL (Section-7 Lot-5)

Children:

2.3005	i.	Florence Ludlow	(1891-1893)
2.3006	ii.	+ Helen Ludlow	
2.3007	iii.	+ Albert Ludlow	
2.3008	iv.	+ Edmund Ludlow	
2.3009	v.	+ Mildred Ludlow	

2.3006 Helen 5 Ludlow *(Samuel4 James3 James2 Israel1)*
　　　　　b. 1895 Aug 14, Paxton, IL
　　　　　d. 1982 Nov 07, Hinsdale, IL
　　　　　bur: Glen Cemetery, Paxton, IL (Section-7 Lot-5)

　　　　　m. Elon Archibald Messenger, 1918 Oct 10, Paxton, IL
　　　　　b. 1891 Dec 12, Patoka, IL
　　　　　d. 1941 Sep 17, Hinsdale, IL
　　　　　bur: Glen Cemetery, Paxton, IL (Section-7 Lot-5)

　　　　　Son of George W. and Augusta Messenger.
Graduate of Illinois State Normal University, 1913.

Children:

2.4007 i.　　+ James Ludlow Messenger
2.4008 ii.　　+ Martha Messenger
2.4009 iii.　 + Archie Allen Messenger
2.4010 iv.　　+ Adele Messenger

2.4007 James Ludlow 6 Messenger *(Helen5 Samuel4 James3 James2 Israel1)*
　　　　　b. 1919 Aug 28, Champaign, IL
　　　　　d. 1956 Oct 17, Philipsburg, PA
　　　　　bur: ---

　　　　　m. Coleen Melton, 1945 Mar 31, Arlington, VA
　　　　　b. 1920 Sep 29, Gaffney, SC
　　　　　d. 2014 Jul 27, Granville, OH
　　　　　bur: ---

Coleen married 2nd Robert Pitt (1922-2014) and her children were legally
adopted by him. Together they raised Ann Pitt, Robert's daughter from a
previous marriage.

Children: @- Robert's daughter from a previous marriage

2.5021 i.　　+ Susan Messenger
2.5022 ii.　　+ Martha Messenger
2.5023 iii.　 + James Ludlow Messenger, Jr.
2.5024 iv.@ + Ann Pitt

2.5021 Susan 7 Messenger *(James7 Helen5 Samuel4 James3 James 2 Israel1)*
   b. 1948, OH

   m1 Roy Tiede

   m2 Gregg Oehler, 1981 Aug 22, Boston, MA

Children(m2):

2.6028 i.　+ Jeffrey Oehler　　　　　b. 1983, NY

2.5022 Martha "Marcie" 7 Messenger *(James6 Helen5 Samuel4 James3 James2 Israel1)*
   b. 1950, OH

   m. Corvis Steven Catsouphes, 1975 Nov 30, Ipswich, MA
   b. 1948, NY

   Son of Aristotle Catsouphes and Beatrice (Jampalis) Catsouphes.

Children:

2.6029 i.　+ Marcus Catsouphes
2.6030 ii.　Jaymeson Catsouphes　　　b. 1986, MA

2.6029 Marcus 8 Catsouphes *(Martha7 James6 Helen5 Samuel4 James3 James2 Israel1)*
   b. 1982, MA

   m. Kristen "Kristy" Allenby, 2013 Sep 28, Newport, RI
   b. 1982, CT

Children:

2.7021 i.　Sloane Elizabeth Catsouphes　　b. 2015, MA

2.5023 James Ludlow 7 Messenger Jr. *(James6 Helen5 Samuel4 James3 James2 Israel1)*
   b. 1956

   m. Patricia Peterson, 1989 Jun 18

Children:

2.6031 i.　James Ludlow Messenger III
2.6032 ii.　Laura Messenger

2.5024 Ann Pitt

    m. Roger Waldon

Children:

2.6033 i.   Matthew Waldon
2.6034 ii.   Christopher Waldon
2.6035 iii. + Emily Waldon

2.6035 Emily Waldon

    m. William "Will" Costigan III

Children:

2.7022 i.   Liam Costigan

2.4008 Martha 6 Messenger *(Helen5 Samuel4 James3 James2 Israel1)*
    b. 1921, CO

    m. Harvey Edward Thomas, 1944 Jun 24, Hinsdale, IL
    b. 1921 Feb 09, Chicago, IL
    d. 2014 Sep 06, Northport, MI[liii]
    bur: unk

Children:

2.5025 i. + Timothy Kehl Thomas
2.5026 ii. + Katherine Thomas
2.5027 iii. + Theodore Elon Thomas
2.5028 iv. + Rachel Thomas
2.5029 v. + Louise Thomas

2.5025 Timothy Kehl 7 Thomas *(Martha6 Helen5 Samuel4 James3 James2 Israel1)*
    b. 1947, MI

    m1 Monica Wyatt, 1970, Geneva, IL (div., 1986)
    m2 Paula Dean Keith, 1989, Tinley Park, IL (div., 2009)

Children(m1):

2.6036 i. + Matthew Kehl Thomas
2.6037 ii.   Abigail Leigh Thomas   b. 1983, WI

Children(m2):

2.6038 iii.   Charity Christian Thomas   b. 1995, TN

2.6036 Matthew Kehl 8 Thomas *(Timothy7 Martha6 Helen5 Samuel4 James3 James2 Israel1)*
        b. 1970, IL

        m. Angela DeWitt, 1992, Palos Hills, IL

Children:

2.7023 i.   Wyatt Benjamin Thomas   b. 1998
2.7024 ii.   Molly Elizabeth Thomas   b. 2001
2.7025 iii.   John Matthew Thomas   b. 2004

2.5026 Katherine 9 Thomas *(Martha6 Helen5 Samuel4 James3 James2 Israel1)*
        b. 1950 Jan 13, Elyria, OH
        d. 2012 Oct 28, Chattanooga, TN
        bur: unk

        m. Paul Fabin, 1972 Aug 19, Hinsdale, IL (div)

Children: @-adopted

2.6039 i. @ Joel Thomas Fabin   b. 1978, IL

2.5027 Theodore Elon 7 Thomas *(Martha6 Helen5 Samuel4 James3 James2 Israel1)*
        b. 1954, IL

        m1 Laura Leigh Gregory, 1975 Jun 21, Naperville, IL
        m2 Jill Marie Bruhschwein, 2009

Children(m1):

2.6040 i.   Heather Leigh Thomas   b. 1978, IL
2.6041 ii.   +   Erik Elon Thomas
2.6042 iii.   Summer Leigh Thomas   b. 1986, IL
2.6043 iv.   Adam Gregory Thomas   b. 1990, IL

Children(m2): @ step-children from wife's previous marriage

2.6044 v. @ +   Richard Brady Walen
2.6045 vi. @ +   Erin Marie Walen
2.6046 vii.@ +   Jared Matthew Walen

35

2.6041 Erik Elon 8 Thomas *(Theodore7 Marth6 Helen5 Samuel4 James3 James2 Israel1)*
       b. 1982, IL

       m. Hannah Lee Furman, 2011, MI
       b. 1987, MI

Children:

| 2.7026 i. | Fionna Lee Thomas | b. 2008, MI |
| 2.7027 ii. | Lydia Lee Thomas | b. 2014, MI |

2.6044 Richard Brady Walen
       b. 1982, IL

       m. Jessica Pickul, 2006

Children:

| 2.7028 i. | Piper James Walen | b. 2014, OH |

2.6045 Erin Marie Walen
       b. 1984, IL

       m. John Daniel Keclick, 2008, IL

Children:

| 2.7029 i. | Dean Jeremy Keclick | b. 2013, WI |

2.6046 Jared Matthew Walen
       b. 1986, IL

       m. Holly Marie Weikal, 2014, IL

2.5028 Rachel 7 Thomas *(Martha6 Helen5 Samuel4 James3 James2 Israel1)*
       b. 1958, IL

       m. Donald Joseph Guzior, 1986 Jul 12, Naperville, IL (div)
       b. 1960

       Son of Joseph and Betty Guzior.

Children:

2.6047	i.	Kyle Thomas Guzior	b. 1990, IL
2.6048	ii.	Rebecca Thomas Guzior	b. 1995, IL
2.6049	iii.	Joseph Thomas Guzior	b. 1997, IL

2.5029 Louise 7 Thomas *(Martha6 Helen5 Samuel4 James3 James2 Israel1)*
      b. 1960, IL

      m. Steven Raymond Leuthner, 1987 Sep 19, Hinsdale, IL
      b. 1963, IL

      Son of Edward and Delores Leuthner.

Children:

2.6050	i.	Tess Catherine Leuthner	b. 1990, IL
2.6051	ii.	Martha Claire Leuthner	b. 1992, IL
2.6052	iii.	Jonathan Edward Leuthner	b. 1995, IL

2.4009 Archie Allen 6 Messenger *(Helen5 Samuel4 James3 James2 Israel1)*
      b. 1923, CO

U.S. Navy Air Corps fighter pilot (LTJG), 1942-1945; Amherst College, B.A. in Economics, 1945; University of Michigan Law School, LLB, 1950. Attorney with Union Carbide Corp.; elected to the USATF Masters Hall of Fame in 2001.[liv]

      m1 Elizabeth Barss, 1951 May 05, Riverside, IL
      b. 1927 Aug 30, Ann Arbor, MI
      d. 1988 Mar 04, Plymouth, NH
      bur: Waterville Valley, NH

      m2 Jane Ashton, 1990 Aug 11
      b. 1924 Oct 17, New York, NY
      d. 2014 Jul 13, Albany, NY

Children(m1):

2.5030	i.	+ John Barss Messenger	
2.5031	ii.	+ Elizabeth Messenger	
2.5032	iii.	Paul Ludlow Messenger	(1957)
2.5033	iv.	+ Andrew Archie Messenger	
2.5034	v.	+ Helen Messenger	
2.5035	vi.	+ Heather Messenger	

2.5030 John Barss 7 Messenger *(Archie6 Helen5 Samuel4 James3 James2 Israel1)*
　　　　b. 1952, IL

Amherst College, B.A. in English, 1974; Pace University School of Law, J.D., 1979. Attorney with various telecommunication companies in New York, NY; Washington, DC; Boston, MA and Rochester, NY. [iv]

　　　　m. Judith Marie Williams, 1977 Jun 04, Danbury, CT
　　　　b. 1952, CT

Children:

2.6053 i.	Geoffrey Anson Messenger	b. 1980
2.6054 ii.	James Andrew Messenger	(1981-2012)
2.6055 iii. +	Charles Roderick Messenger	

2.6055 Charles Roderick 8 Messenger *(John7 Archibald6 Helen5 Samuel4 James3 James2 Israel1)*
　　　　b. 1985

　　　　m. Sarah Hunter, 2013 Jul 21
　　　　b. 1988, NJ

2.5031 Elizabeth 7 Messenger *(Archie6 Helen5 Samuel4 James3 James2 Israel1)*
　　　　b. 1954, IL

　　　　m. William Edward Johns, 1982 May 15, Larchmont, NY
　　　　b. 1956, NY

Children:

2.6056 i. +	Scott William Johns	
2.6057 ii.	Lisa Noelle Johns	b. 1987, FL
2.6058 iii.	Keith Allen Johns	b. 1989, FL

2.6056 Scott William 8 Johns *(Elizabeth7 Archie6 Helen5 Samuel4 James3 James2 Israel1)*
　　　　b. 1985, FL

　　　　m. Sara Elisabeth Gomez, 2010 Jan 23, San Salvador, El Salvador
　　　　b. 1987, El Salvador

2.5033 Andrew Archie 7 Messenger *(Archie6 Helen5 Samuel4 James3 James2 Israel1)*
　　　　b. 1959, IL

m Barbara Ross English, 1989 Jul 14 (div.)
b. 1958

Children:

2.6059 i.	Amanda Elizabeth Messenger	b. 1990
2.6060 ii.	Daniel Ames Messenger	b. 1990
2.6061 iii.	Nora English Messenger	b. 1993
2.6062 iv.	Peter Hyanno Messenger	b. 1999

2.5034 Helen 7 Messenger *(Archie6 Helen5 Samuel4 James3 James2 Israel1)*
b. 1960, IL

m1 Mark Gilson (div.)
m2 Moe Branch

2.5035 Heather 7 Messenger *(Archie6 Helen5 Samuel4 James3 James2 Israel1)*
b. 1964, NY

Children:

2.6063 i.	Andrew Edward Messenger	b. 2000, FL[lvi]

2.4010 Adele 6 Messenger *(Helen5 Samuel4 James3 James2 Israel1)*
b. 1927, CO

m. James Frank Mayer, 1950 Dec 30, Hinsdale, IL
b. 1926 Oct 05, Oak Park, IL
d. 2012 Nov 17, IL
bur: Mount Emblem Cemetery, Elmhurst, IL

Son of Frank and Bessie Mayer.

Children: @-adopted

2.5036 i. @	James Frank Mayer, Jr.	b. 1957, IL
2.5037 ii. @ +	Amy Mayer	
2.5038 iii.@ +	Cynthia Mayer	

2.5037 Amy Mayer
b. 1959, IL

m. Jan Wilking, 1985 Aug 25, Park City, UT (div. 1990)

Children:

2.6064 i.   + Katie Wilking

2.6064 Katie Wilking
      b. 1986, UT

      m. Marc Richard Clinard, 2014 Aug 08, Park City, UT
      b. 1981, SD

2.5038 Cynthia Mayer
      b. 1964, IL

      m. Duncan Cuyler Smith, 1990 Oct 07, Hinsdale, IL
      b. 1964, CT

Children:

2.6065 i.	Connor Ealing Smith	b. 1993, IL
2.6066 ii.	Grace Annabelle Smith	b. 1996, IN

2.3007 Albert 5 Ludlow *(Samuel4 James3 James2 Israel1)*
      b. 1897 Apr 26, Paxton, IL
      d. 1962 May 18
      bur: Glen Cemetery, Paxton, IL

      m. Cora Dot (Baker) Joseph, 1949 Jun 30, Kankakee, IL
      b. 1890 Jun --, Kankakee, IL
      d. 1966 Nov 03, Kankakee, IL
      bur: Mound Grove Cemetery, Kankakee, IL

2.3008 Edmund 5 Ludlow *(Samuel4 James3 James2 Israel1)*
      b. 1902 Jul 24, Paxton, IL
      d. 1976 Dec 20, Columbus, IN
      bur: Garland Brook Cemetery, Columbus, IN (Section-37 Lot-138)

      m. Kathryn Jane Dunnan, 1927 Apr 30, Knightstown, IN
      b. 1904 May 06, Paxton, IL
      d. 1992 Feb 12, Columbus, IN
      bur: Garland Brook Cemetery, Columbus, IN (Section-37 Lot-138)

Children:

2.4011 i.   Edmund Dunnan Ludlow

2.4011 Edmund Dunnan 6 Ludlow *(Edmund5 Samuel4 James3 James2 Israel1)*
   b. 1928, IN

   m. Lois Virginia Aders, 1952 Sep 20, Corpus Christi, TX
   b. 1929, IN

Children:

2.5039 i.   +   Mark Edmund Ludlow
2.5040 ii.   +   Lynn Kathleen Ludlow
2.5041 iii. +   James Brian Ludlow

2.5039 Mark Edmund 7 Ludlow *(Edmund6 Edmund5 Samuel4 James3 James2 Israel1)*
   b. 1954, Bermuda

   m. Judith Anne Lamia, 1988 Sep 18
   b. 1960, NY

Children:

2.6067 i.   Scott Madison Ludlow   b. 1996, FL

2.5040 Lynn Kathleen 7 Ludlow *(Edmund6 Edmund5 Samuel4 James3 James2 Israel1)*
   b. 1957, VA

   m. Robert Aleksov, 1993 Oct 02, Columbus, IN

Children:

2.6068 i.   Kathryn Ann Aleksov   b. 1993, IN

2.5041 James Brian 7 Ludlow *(Edmund6 Edmund5 Samuel4 James3 James2 Israel1)*
   b. 1959, VA

   m. Sandra Erica Supstiks, 1986 Oct 04, Des Moines, IA
   b. 1962, IA

Children:

2.6069 i.   Alexander James Ludlow   b. 1991, IL
2.6070 ii.   Mackenzie Erica Ludlow   b. 1993, IL
2.6071 iii.   Madison Kathryn Ludlow   b. 1993, IL

2.3009 Mildred 5 Ludlow *(Samuel4 James3 James2 Israel1)*
> b. 1908 Mar 08, Paxton, IL
> d. 2008 Apr 09, Scottsdale, AZ
> bur: Osmond Cemetery, Osmond, NE
>
> m. Clarence William "Clare" Riessen, 1932 Aug 16, Osmond, NE
> b. 1909 Jul 28, Osmond, NE
> d. 1990 May 12, Ojai, CA
> bur: Osmond Cemetery, Osmond, NE

Son of Claus Riessen and Luelia Georgina (Mahrt) Riessen. Tennis coach at Northwestern University, 1959-75, winning a Big 10 championship, 1963.[lvii]

Children:

2.4012 i.   + Susan Ludlow Riessen
2.4013 ii.   + Martin Clare Riessen

2.4012 Susan Ludlow 6 Riessen *(Mildred5 Samuel4 James3 James2 Israel1)*
> b. 1939 Oct 28, Yuma, AZ
>
> m. David Henderson, 1961 Dec 30,
> b. 1938 Oct 28, Des Moines, IA
> d. 1993 Sep 01, Des Moines, IA
> bur: Resthaven Cemetery, West Des Moines, IA

Son of George Henderson and Ruth Alma (Gusland) Henderson.

Children:

2.5042 i.   + Lance David Henderson
2.5043 ii.   + Tanya Kay Henderson

2.5042 Lance David 7 Henderson *(Susan6 Mildred5 Samuel4 James3 James2 Israel1)*
> b. 1963, IA
>
> m. Ann Meany, 1990 Mar 17, Chicago, IL

Children:

2.6072	i.	Siena Marie Henderson	b. 1994, IL
2.6073	ii.	Nyasa Ann Henderson	b. 1996, MN

2.5043 Tanya Kay 7 Henderson *(Susan6 Mildred5 Samuel4 James3 James2 Israel1)*
b. 1966, IA

m. Richard Reed, 1993 Nov 24, Chicago, IL (div.)

Children:

2.6074	i.	Jazzmin Davi Reed	b. 1994, IL
2.6075	ii.	Morgan Bailey Reed	b. 1997, AZ

2.4013 Martin Clare 6 Riessen *(Mildred5 Samuel4 James3 James2 Israel1)*
b. 1941, IL

Played collegiate tennis at Northwestern University, reaching the NCAA Singles finals three times. He was a member of the U.S. Davis Cup team for several years between 1963 and 1981; won six singles titles in the Open Era and also reached the quarterfinals in singles at both the Australian Open and the U.S. Open in 1971. He won 53 doubles titles, including the U.S. Open in 1976 and the French Open in 1971 with Arthur Ashe, and reached the doubles final at the U.S. Open in 1975 & 1978; the Australian Open, 1971 and Wimbledon, 1969.[lviii]

m1 Sally Lybek, 1964 Dec 19 (div. 1976)

m2 April Melinda Satow, 1977 Jan 26, Santa Barbara, CA
b. 1945, MN

Children (m2):

2.5044	i.	+	Jennifer Michele Riessen
2.5045	ii.	+	Cristina Elizabeth Riessen

2.5044 Jennifer Michele 7 Riessen *(Martin6 Mildred5 Samuel4 James3 James2 Israel1)*
b. 1978, CA

m. John Trelor Rickard III, 2008 Aug 09, Santa Barbara Co., CA
b. 1977, OR

Son of John Trelor Rickard II and Nikki Rickard.

Children:

2.6076	i.	Samantha Riessen Rickard	b. 2009, CA
2.6077	ii.	John Trelor Rickard IV	b. 2012, CA

2.5045 Cristina Elizabeth 7 Riessen *(Martin6 Mildred5 Samuel4 James3 James2 Israel1)*
b. 1980, CA

m. Cristopher Kelly Broderick, 2006 Sep 30, Santa Barbara, CA
b. 1976, NY

Son of Jon and Margie Broderick.

Children:

2.6078 i. Catherine Masayo Broderick   b. 2008, England
2.6079 ii. Jack Riessen Broderick   b. 2010, CT

2.2006 Theresa 4 Ludlow *(James3 James2 Israel1)*
b. 1867 Jun 03, Harwood, IL
d. 1954 Mar 11, Indianapolis, IN[lix]
bur: Crown Hill Cemetery, Indianapolis, IN (Section-60 Lot-842)

m. John Lee Benedict, 1890 Jun 26
b. 1862 Oct 11, Rantoul, IL
d. 1940 Jul 05, Muncie, IN
bur: Crown Hill Cemetery, Indianapolis, IN (Section-60 Lot-842)

Son of John Ashman Benedict. Graduated DePauw University, 1887. Attorney and member of the Indiana State Legislature.

Children:

2.3010 i. + Paul Ludlow Benedict
2.3011 ii. + Howard Middlecoff Benedict
2.3012 iii. + Katherine Benedict

2.3010 Paul Ludlow 5 Benedict *(Theresa4 James3 James2 Israel1)*
b. 1891 Dec 20, IN
d. 1954 Mar 24, Rochelle, IL[lx]
bur: Forest Hill Cemetery, Greencastle, IN

D.D., DePauw University; Chaplain during WWI and WWII; Methodist minister.

m. Marian McCullough Ostrom, 1913 Dec 16
b. 1889 Dec 25, Milwaukee, WI
d. 1960 Feb 10, Jackson Co., OR
bur: Forest Hill Cemetery, Greencastle, IN

Children: @-adopted

2.4014 i. @   Paul Corwin Benedict   (1926-1993)
2.4015 ii. @ + Mary Jane Benedict

2.4015 Mary Jane Benedict
      b. 1928, KY

      m. John Richard Dellenback, 1948 Sep 10
      b. 1918 Nov 06, Chicago, IL
      d. 2002 Dec 07, Medford, OR
      bur: unk

      Son of William and Margaret (Albright) Dellenback. Earned his B.S.
Degree from Yale University, 1940, and afterward attended the Northwestern
University School of Speech and University Of Michigan Law School. He served
in the United States Navy between 1942-1946, followed by service in the
United States Naval Reserve.
He was a delegate to the Republican National Conventions in 1964, 1968 and
1972, and a member of the Oregon state legislature from 1960 until 1966.
He was elected to Congress, serving 1967-1975. He was the Associate Director
of the United States Peace Corp, 1975-1977, and president of the Christian
College Coalition, 1977-1988.[lxi]

Children:

2.5046 i.   Richard Ludlow Dellenback
2.5047 ii.   David Albright Dellenback
2.5048 iii.   Barbara Clare Dellenback

2.3011 Howard Middlecoff 5 Benedict *(Theresa4 James3 James2 Israel1)*
      b. 1893 Jul 06, Indianapolis, IN
      d. 1923 Mar 12, Indianapolis, IN
      bur: Crown Hill Cemetery, Indianapolis, IN (Section-60 Lot-842)

      m. Ruth Overbaugh, 1921 Oct 21, Ridgewood, NJ
      b. 1896 Feb 25, Kingston, NY
      d. 1986 Mar 16, Cuyahoga Co., OH
      bur: Crown Hill Cemetery, Indianapolis, IN (Section-60 Lot-842)

Children:

2.4016 i.   + John David Benedict

2.4016 John David 6 Benedict *(Howard5 Theresa4 James3 James2 Israel1)*

b. 1922, IN

Graduate of Renssalaer Polytechnic Institute, 1949. Served in the US Air Force during WWII. President of the Industrial Relations Association of Detroit.

m. Mary Catherine Gustafson, 1950 Aug 07, Cleveland Heights, OH
b. 1926, OH

Children:

2.5049 i.		Steven Ludlow Benedict	b. 1952, MI
2.5050 ii.	+	Ruth Lee Benedict	
2.5051 iii.	+	Paul David Benedict	
2.5052 iv.		Alan Edgar Benedict	b. 1962, MI

2.5050 Ruth Lee 7 Benedict *(John6 Howard5 Theresa4 James3 James2 Israel1)*

b. 1954, MI

m. Jonas Taub, 1983 Feb 19
b. 1950, NY

Son of Abraham and Haddasah (Friedman) Taub

Children:

2.6080 i.	Emily Benedict Taub	b. 1988, NH
2.6081 ii.	Aaron David Taub	b. 1992, NH

2.5051 Paul David 7 Benedict *(John6 Howard5 Theresa4 James3 James2 Israel1)*

b. 1957 May 17, MI

m. Susan Diane Capaldo
b. 1966, OH

Children:

2.6082 i.	Elizabeth Rose Benedict	b. 1994, MI

2.3012 Katherine ₅ Benedict *(Theresa4 James3 James2 Israel1)*
    b. 1896 Nov 20, Indianapolis, IN
    d. 1989 Dec 22, Muncie, IN
    bur: Elm Ridge Memorial Park, Muncie, IN

    m. Claude Earl Palmer, 1919 June 19, Indianapolis, IN
    b. 1886 Dec 01, Spring Green, WI
    d. 1945 Feb 01, Cleveland, OH
    bur: Elm Ridge Memorial Park, Muncie, IN

    Son of William Palmer and Lucy Lucretia (Bonham) Palmer.

Children:

2.4017 i.   William Benedict Palmer   (1920)
2.4018 ii.   +   Marian Palmer
2.4019 iii.   +   Howard Benedict Palmer

2.4017 Marian ₆ Palmer *(Katherine5 Theresa4 James3 James2 Israel1)*
    b. 1922, IN

    m. Samuel Starbuck Banta, 1946
    b. 1918 Aug 16, Muncie, IN
    d. 1998 Aug 06, Muncie, IN
    bur: Elm Ridge Memorial Park, Muncie, IN

    Son of John F. and Lucille Banta. Graduate of Ball State University.

Children: @- adopted

2.5053 i. @ Samuel Palmer Banta   b. 1955

2 .4019 Howard Benedict ₆ Palmer *(Katherine5 Theresa4 James3 James2 Israel1)*
    b. 1925, IN

B.S., Carnegie Tech.; PH.D., University of Wisconsin. Professor
at Penn State College.

    m1 Katherine Douglas Watson, 1951 Jun 30, Waupaca, WI[lxii]
    b. 1928, Canada
    d. 2009 Oct 01,
    bur: unk

Children:

2.5054 i.   Andrew Stuart Palmer   b. 1952
2.5055 ii.   + Jeffrey Howard Palmer
2.5056 iii.   David James Palmer

2.5055 Jeffrey Howard 7 Palmer *(Howard6 Katherine5 Theresa4 James3 James2 Israel1)*
        b. 1954

        m. Carol Ann Bray, 1983 Oct 15

Children:

2.6083 i.   Justin Patrick Palmer   b. 1988
2.6084 ii.   Christopher James Palmer   b. 1991

2.5056 David James 7 Palmer *(Howard6 Katherine5 Theresa4 James3 James2 Israel1)*
        b. 1957

        m. Sara Harding, 1986 Feb 22

Children:

2.6085 i.   Steven James Palmer   b. 1989

2.2007 Edmund 4 Ludlow *(James3 James2 Israel1)*
        b. 1870 Feb 20, Harwood, IL
        d. 1903 Apr 05, Los Angeles, CA
        bur: Glen Cemetery, Paxton, IL (Section-7 Lot-5)

"Edmund Ludlow, M.D., Northwestern University Medical School, Chicago, 1895, formerly intern at St. Luke's Hospital, Chicago, and at the Central Indiana Hospital for the Insane, Indianapolis, who left his home in Paxton, Ill., in search of health, going first to Silverton, Colo., and then to Los Angeles, died in the latter city April 5 [1903]." [lxiii]

2.2009 Katherine "Kitty" 4 Ludlow *(James3 James2 Israel1)*
- b. 1877 May 20, Harwood, IL
- d. 1952 Mar 14, Paxton, IL
- bur: Glen Cemetery, Paxton, IL

m. William Howard White, 1898 March 17, Indianapolis, IN
- b. 1876 Mar 17, Paxton, IL
- d. 1931 Mar 07, Paxton, IL[lxiv]
- bur: Glen Cemetery, Paxton, IL

Son of Thomas Jefferson White and Mary Jane (Kelly) White.

Children:

2.3013	i.	+	Dorothy Ludlow White
2.3014	ii.	+	Theresa White
2.3015	iii.	+	Katherine White
2.3016	iv.	+	William Ludlow White
2.3017	v.	+	Mary Charlotte White

2.3013 Dorothy Ludlow 5 White *(Katharine 4 James3 James2 Israel1)*
- b. 1899 Mar 03, Paxton, IL
- d. 1976 Sep 16, Santa Fe, NM
- bur: Glen Cemetery, Paxton, IL

m. Dewey Frank Fagerburg, 1920 Dec 22, Chicago, Cook Co., IL
- b. 1898 Jul 25, Eliot, IL
- d. 1958 Jun 13, Hinsdale, IL
- bur: Glen Cemetery, Paxton, IL

Son of Edward H. Fagerburg and Charlotte (Andersson) Fagerburg.

Chicago lawyer; member of Sigma Alpha Epsilon's National Law Committee. Practiced law as a partner of the firm of Nicholson, Crandall and Snyder.[lxv]

Children:

2.4020	i.	+	Charlotte Fagerburg
2.4021	ii.	+	Dewey Frank Fagerburg, Jr.
2.4022	iii.	+	Karin Fagerburg

2.4020 Charlotte 6 Fagerburg *(Dorothy5 Katharine 4 James3 James2 Israel1)*
　　　　　b. 1924 Dec 26, Evanston, IL
　　　　　d. 1990 Jul 15, Rochester, NY
　　　　　bur: c

　　　　　m. Leonard Thomas Smith, 1946 Sep 07
　　　　　b. 1922 Mar 01, Margaret, TX
　　　　　d. 2003 May 29, Stuart, FL
　　　　　bur: c

　　　　　Son of Roscoe Leonard Smith and Tennie Elizabeth (Linn) Smith.

Children:

2.5057 i.　　+　Dorothy Lynn Smith
2.5058 ii.　 +　Andrew Dunlop Smith
2.5059 iii.　+　Katherine Ludlow Smith
2.5060 iv.　 +　Theresa Anne Smith

2.5057 Dorothy Lynn 7 Smith *(Charlotte6 Dorothy5 Katharine 4 James3 James2 Israel1)*
　　　　　b. 1947, IL

　　　　　m1 Ronald Paul Leroy, 1967
　　　　　b. 1946 Sep 19, NY
　　　　　d. 1997 Apr 14, CA
　　　　　bur: Pleasanton Memorial Gardens, Alameda, CA

　　　　　m2 Jeffrey Alan Turner, 2001 Feb 18, Danville, CA

Children(m1):

2.6086 i.　　+　Thomas Harvey Leroy
2.6087 ii.　 +　Daniel William Leroy

2.6086 Thomas Harvey 8 Leroy *(Dorothy7 Charlotte6 Dorothy5 Katharine 4 James3 James2 Israel1)*

　　　　　m. Susan Taylor

Children:

2.7030 i.　　　Bowen Thomas Leroy
2.7031 ii.　　 Sylvan Taylor Leroy

2.6087 Daniel William 8 Leroy *(Dorothy7 Charlotte6 Dorothy5 Katharine 4 James3 James2 Israel1)*

m. Kim Jankow

Children:

2.7032 i.   Cameron Thomas Leroy

2.5058 Andrew Dunlop 7 Smith *(Charlotte6 Dorothy5 Katharine 4 James3 James2 Israel1)*
b. 1960

m. Sandra Minton, 1984 Jun 16

Children:

| 2.6088 i. | Charlotte Smith | b. 1994 |
| 2.6089 ii. | Barrett Smith | b. 1997 |

2.5059 Katherine Ludlow 7 Smith *(Charlotte6 Dorothy5 Katharine 4 James3 James2 Israel1)*

m. Stephen Ware, 1994 Jun (div, 2013)

Children:

| 2.6090 i. | Adam Jordan Ware | b.1996 |
| 2.6091 ii. | Spencer Ware | b. 2002 |

2.5060 Theresa Anne 7 Smith *(Charlotte6 Dorothy5 Katharine4 James3 James2 Israel1)*

m. Jerry Livadas, 1979

Children:

| 2.6092 i. | Nicholas Livadas | b. 1979 |
| 2.6093 ii. | + Adrienne Therese Livadas | b. 1984 |

2.6093 Adrienne Therese 8 Livadas *(Theresa7 Charlotte6 Dorothy5 Katharine4 James3 James2 Israel1)*

m. Brandon Tate

Children:

| 2.7033 i. | Alexander Nathan Tate | b. 2011 |
| 2.7034 ii. | Jameson Grant Tate | b. 2013 |

2.4021 Dewey Frank 6 Fagerburg, Jr. *(Dorothy5 Katharine4 James3 James2 Israel1)*
b. 1929 Jan 12, Evanston, IL

m1 Rachel Allen, 1951 Sep 01, Garden City, NJ

m2 Joan Marie Kasick

Children:

2.5061	i.	+	Karin Fagerburg
2.5062	ii.	+	Anne Fagerburg
2.5063	iii.	+	Ruth Fagerburg
2.5064	iv.	+	Rachel Fagerburg
2.5065	v.	+	Sarah Fagerburg

2.5061 Karin 7 Fagerburg *(Dewey6 Dorothy5 Katharine4 James3 James2 Israel1)*
b. 1952

2.5062 Anne 7 Fagerburg *(Dewey6 Dorothy5 Katharine4 James3 James2 Israel1)*
b. 1954

m. Morris Jacob

2.5063 Ruth 7 Fagerburg *(Dewey6 Dorothy5 Katharine4 James3 James2 Israel1)*
b. 1955

m. Frederick A. Schipsky
b. 1952, Canada

"Graduated from the University of British Columbia in 1974 with a Bachelor of Music degree in composition. Attended graduate school at Juilliard School, 1974-76. Served as double bassist with the Vancouver Symphony.
Among his compositions was "Fanfare to the Royal Visit" performed at the British Columbia Place Stadium in the presence of Queen Elizabeth."

Children:

2.6094	i.	Anton Schipsky
2.6095	ii.	Paul Schipsky

2.5064 Rachel 7 Fagerburg *(Dewey6 Dorothy5 Katharine4 James3 James2 Israel1)*
  b. 1957

  m. Richard Menaul
  b. 1953 Dec 28, Chicago, IL
  d. 2013 Jul 23, Medfield, MA[lxvi]
  bur: unk

  Son of Richard Menaul and Mary (O'Neill) Menaul. Bachelor of Music
degree, Ithaca College; Master of Music degree, Northwestern University;
Member of the Boston Ballet Orchestra, the Boston Pops Esplanade Orchestra,
the Handel & Haydn Society. Appeared with the Boston Symphony
Orchestra.[lxvii]

Children:

2.6096 i. Leah Catherine Menaul b. 1995

2.5065 Sarah 7 Fagerburg *(Dewey6 Dorothy5 Katharine4 James3 James2 Israel1)*
  b. 1964

  m. Brian Thomas Nixon

Children:

2.6097 i. Catherine Allen Nixon b. 1992
2.5098 ii. Brian Thomas Nixon, Jr. b. 1993
2.6099 iii. Hannah Elizabeth Nixon b. 1998

2.4022 Karin 6 Fagerburg *(Dorothy5 Katharine4 James3 James2 Israel1)*
  b. 1932

  m. David Wemyss Jackson, 1953

Children:

2.5066 i. + George Dewey Jackson
2.5067 ii. + Sue Katherine Jackson
2.5068 iii. + Christine Elizabeth Jackson
2.5069 iv. + Ann Lee Jackson

2.5066 George Dewey 7 Jackson *(Karin6 Dorothy5 Katharine4 James3 James2 Israel1)*

m. Eva -----

Children:

2.6100 i.	Nate Jackson	b. 1985
2.6101 ii.	Julia Jackson	b. 1989

2.5067 Sue Katherine "Sukie" 7 Jackson *(Karin6 Dorothy5 Katharine4 James3 James2 Israel1)*
b. 1956

m. Robert Tanabe

Children:

2.6102 i.	Kenji Tanabe	b. 1989
2.6103 ii.	Mari Tanabe	b. 1991
2.6104 iii.	Kimiko Tanabe	b. 1994

2.5068 Christine Elizabeth 7 Jackson *(Karin6 Dorothy5 Katharine4 James3 James2 Israel1)*
b. 1958

m. Yak Jakobs

Children:

2.6105 i.	Anna Jakobs

2.5069 Ann Lee 7 Jackson *(Karin6 Dorothy5 Katharine4 James3 James2 Israel1)*

m. Doug Erwin

Children:

2.6106 i.	Monika Erwin	b. 1989
2.6107 ii.	Kari Erwin	b. 1992
2.6108 iii.	Mike Erwin	b. 1994

2.3014 Theresa 5 White *(Katharine4 James3 James2 Israel1)*

> b. 1901 Jun 28, Paxton, IL
> d. 1975 Dec 14, Virginia, MN
> bur: Memorial Park Cemetery, Skokie, IL
>
> m. William Oats Jeffery III, 1928 Jul 26, Evanston, IL
> b. 1896 Jun 08, Soudan, MN
> d.1953 Dec 07, Evanston, IL
> bur: Memorial Park Cemetery, Skokie, IL

Son of William Oats Jeffery, Jr. and Ellen (Richards) Jeffery.
His father, William Oats Jeffery, Jr., established the family business, IRMCO
(International Refining and Manufacturing Company) in Evanston, Illinois, in
1914, which remains their family business to the present day.
His grandfather, William Oats Jeffery (1841-1891) of Cornwall, England, was a
mining engineer who immigrated to the United States and settled in
Minnesota.

Children: @-stepchild, daughter of Mr. Jeffery's by a previous marriage

2.4023 i. @ + Barbara Ann Jeffery
2.4024 ii.   + Elizabeth Jane Jeffery
2.4025 iii.   + Jeannette Jeffery
2.4026 iv.   + William Oats Jeffery IV

2.4023 Barbara Ann Jeffery

> b. 1925
>
> m. Edward George Forester, Jr., 1949 Sep 09
> b. 1926 Mar 05, Evanston, IL
> d. 2014 Jul 31, Glenview, IL [lxviii]
> bur: unk

Children:

2.5070	i.	Lynn Ann Forester	
2.5071	ii.	Jane Ellen Forester	
2.5072	iii.	Penny Marie Forester	
2.5073	iv.	Edward George Forester III	(1956-1957)
2.5074	v.	Jeffery Edward Forester	

2.4024 Elizabeth Jane 6 Jeffery *(Theresa5 Katharine4 James3 James2 Israel1)*
b. 1930 Jan 18, Evanston, IL
d. 2007 Jun 07, Corvallis, OR
bur: unk

m. Dana Henderson Storch, 1950 Sep 9
b. 1928 Oct 08, Chicago, IL

Son of Clemens Storch and Olive (Henderson) Storch.

Children:

2.5075 i.   +   Kathryn Ann Storch
2.5076 ii. +   William Dana Storch

2.5075 Kathryn Ann 7 Storch *(Elizabeth6 Theresa5 Katharine4 James3 James2 Israel1)*
b. 1951, IL

m. Robert Dwight Harbaugh, 1975 Jun 17, San Mateo, CA
b. 1952

Children:

2.6109 i.   Erin Elizabeth Harbaugh   b. 1979
2.6110 ii.   Danica Taylor Harbaugh   b. 1981

2.5076 William Dana 7 Storch *(Elizabeth6 Theresa5 Katharine 4 James3 James2 Israel1)*
b. 1953

m1 Sara Power (div.)

m2 Joanne Louise Eimstad, 1990 Jun 15, Benton Co., OR

Children (m1):

2.6111 i.   Trevor Power Storch   b. 1980
2.6112 ii.   Henry Power Storch   b. 1982

2.4025 Jeannette 6 Jeffery *(Theresa5 Katharine4 James3 James2 Israel1)*
>
> b. 1931 Jul 03, Evanston, IL
> d. 2008 Aug 22, Hibbing, MN
> bur: Lakeview Cemetery, Tower, MN
>
> m. John Forest Sweet, 1950 May 24, Crown Point, IN
> b. 1927 Jun 29, Evanston, IL
> d. 2012 Dec 17, Mt. Iron, MN[lxix]
> bur: Lakeview Cemetery, Tower, MN

Son of John Winslow Sweet, Jr. and Harriet (Hopkins) Sweet.
Earned his Bachelor of Science degree in math and physics engineering from Northwestern University in 1951. Served in the U.S. Marine Corps during WWII and was recalled to duty during the Korean War.

Children:

2.5077 i.   + John Forest Sweet, Jr.
2.5078 ii. + Sharlyn Jane Sweet

2.5077 John Forest 7 Sweet, Jr. *(Jeannette6 Theresa5 Katharine4 James3 James2 Israel1)*
>
> b. 1951, IL
>
> m. Debra Jo Berg, 1875 Mar 29, Evanston, IL
> b. 1953

Children:

2.6113 i.   + Jonathan Winslow Sweet
2.6114 ii. + Kyle James Sweet

2.6113 Jonathan Winslow 8 Sweet *(John7 Jeannette6 Theresa5 Katharine4 James3 James2 Israel1)*
>
> b. 1976, IL
>
> m. Lorie Esther Nudel, 2000 Jul 02, Madison, WI
> b. 1975, OH

Children:

2.7035 i.   Jules Eliora Sweet   b. 2004, WI
2.7036 ii. David Sanford Sweet   b. 2011, IL

2.6114 Kyle James 8 Sweet *(John7 Jeannette6 Theresa5 Katharine4 James3 James2 Israel1)*
b. 1980, IL

m. Alice Margaret Stapleton, 2006 Jul15,
b. 1975, DE

Children:

2.7037	i.	Zachary James Sweet	b. 2009, AZ
2.7038	ii.	Zane Christopher Sweet	b. 2011, AZ

2.5078 Sharlyn Jane "Shar" 7 Sweet *(Jeannette6 Theresa5 Katharine4 James3 James2 Israel1)*
b. 1952, NC

Besides being a stay-at-home mom, she has designed and created wedding gowns; costumes for various productions, and more. She appreciates the arts and being outdoors. She and Chuck have traveled on several African safaris and enjoy hunting in Minnesota and Wyoming. [xx]

m. Charles Waldemar "Chuck" Dahl, 1971 Dec 29, Tower, MN
b. 1949, MN

Son of Russell Leroy Dahl and Karin Ingrid (Peterson) Dahl. He made a career in the taconite mining industry, retiring from USS Minntac in June of 2001 as the Agglomerator Maintenance Coordinator. He is an avid sportsman who enjoys hunting and fishing. [xxi]

Children:

2.6115 i. Russell John Dahl
2.6116 ii. Stephen Charles Dahl
2.6117 iii. Timothy James Dahl

2.6115 Russell John 8 Dahl *(Sharlyn7 Jeannette6 Theresa5 Katharine4 James3 James2 Israel1)*
b. 1973, MN

m. Charissa Rae Dimberio, 2000 Apr 15, Virginia, MN
b. 1973, MN

Children:

2.7039	i.	Devyn Lynn Dahl	b. 2001, MN
2.7040	ii.	Derik Russell Dahl	b. 2006, MN

2.6116 Stephen Charles 8 Dahl *(Sharlyn7 Jeannette6 Theresa5 Katharine4 James3 James2 Israel1)*

     b. 1976, MN

     m. Kelly Jo Ross, 2002 Apr 13 (div.)

     (=) Jessica Peterson
     b. 1982

Children(m):

| 2.7041 i. | Brooke Isabella Dahl | b. 2004, MN |
| 2.7042 ii. | Ashley Rae Dahl | b. 2006, MN |

Children(=):

| 2.7043 iii. | Parker Charles Dahl | b. 2013, MN |

2.6117 Timothy James 8 Dahl *(Sharlyn7 Jeannette6 Theresa5 Katharine4 James3 James2 Israel1)*

     b. 1978, MN

     m. Joanna Lyn Maras, 2012 July 26, Prague, Czech Republic[lxxii]
     b. 1984, MN

2.4026 William Oats 6 Jeffery IV *(Theresa5 Katharine4 James3 James2 Israel1)*

     b. 1933 Dec 30, IL
     d. 1989 Sep 29, IL
     bur: Memorial Park Cemetery, Skokie, IL

     m. Janice McKay, 1956 Aug 11
     b. 1936

Children:

2.5079 i.	+	William Charles Jeffery
2.5080 ii.	+	Bradley John Jeffery
2.5081 iii.	+	Anne Jeffery

2.5079 William Charles "Jeff" 7 Jeffery *(William6 Theresa5 Katharine4 James3 James2 Israel1)*

     b. 1957, CA

CEO and current owner of IRMCO (International Refining and Manufacturing Company) in Evanston, Illinois, which recently celebrated one hundred years in business and family ownership (1914-2014).

m1 Kathleen Mary McCarthy, 1982 Oct 09 (div.)

m2 Michelle Scala, 2011 May 20
b. 1972, NJ

Children(m1):

2.6118	i.	+ Kiley Marie Jeffery	
2.6119	ii.	William Charles Jeffery, Jr.	b. 1987, IL
2.6120	iii.	Jenna Maisie Jeffery	b. 1991, IL

2.6118 Kiley Marie Jeffery
b. 1985, IL

m. William Brent "Beau" White, 2011 Sep 10, Glenview, IL

Son of William Brent White and Andrea (Donnellen) White.

Children:

2.7044	i.	Maeve Maudie White	b. 2015

2.5080 Bradley John 7 Jeffery *(William6 Theresa5 Katharine4 James3 James2 Israel1)*
b. 1961

m1 Christine Marie Ettl, 1984 Jun 09
m2 Susan -----, 2007

Children(m1):

2.6121	i.	Courtney Marissa Jeffery	b. 1988
2.6122	ii.	Sydney Leigh Jeffery	b. 1993
2.6123	iii.	Takoda Oats Jeffery	b. 1996

2.5081 Anne 7 Jeffery *(William6 Theresa5 Katharine4 James3 James2 Israel1)*
b. 1968

m. Robert Fitzpatrick, 1992 Nov 27

Children:

2.6124	i.	William John Fitzpatrick	b. 1995
2.6125	ii.	Quinn Jeffery Fitzpatrick	b. 1997
2.6126	iii.	Shane Robert Fitzpatrick	b. 2000

2.3015 Katherine "Kay" 5 White *(Katherine4 James3 James2 Israel1)*
 b. 1903 Mar 07
 d. 1993 Aug 14
 bur: Glen Cemetery, Paxton, IL

 m1 William Davies Mueller
 b. 1898 Feb 12, Graetinger, IA
 d. 1937 Apr 24, Waukegan, IL
 bur: Oak Grove Cemetery, Independence, IA

 m2 Cedric Charles "Ced" Gifford
 b. 1896 Jul 17, Chicago, IL
 d. 1986 Jun 25, Kansas City, MO
 bur: Rosehill Cemetery, Chicago, IL

Children(m1):

2.4027 i.   William Davies Mueller, Jr.   (1928-1937)

Children(m2): @ stepchild, from Mr. Gifford's previous marriage

2.4028 ii. @   Cedric Charles Gifford Jr.

2.3016 William Ludlow "Brud" 5 White *(Katharine4 James3 James2 Israel1)*
 b. 1907 Jun 06
 d. 1991 Oct
 bur: Glen Cemetery, Paxton, IL

2.3017 Mary Charlotte "Shar" 5 White *(Katharine4 James3 James2 Israel1)*
 b. 1914 Dec 15
 d. 2002 Sep 06
 bur: unk

Author of "*Within Adobe Walls : A Santa Fe Journal*" and "*Greatness in the Commonplace : The Art of Boris Gilbertson*".

 m. Howard Marks (div.)
 (=) Boris Gilbertson

2.1003 Charlotte Chambers 3 Ludlow *(James2 Israel1)*
 b. 1824, Hamilton Co., OH
 d. 1879 Jan 13, New Orleans, LA
 bur: Spring Grove Cemetery, Cincinnati, OH (Section-23 Lot-95)

m. Charles Allibone Jones, 1843 Jul 11, "Ludlow Station", OH[lxxiii]
b. 1815 Feb 18, Philadelphia, PA
d. 1851 Jul 04, "Ludlow Station", OH
bur: Spring Grove Cemetery, Cincinnati, OH (Section-23 Lot-95)

Son of George and Esther (Allibone) Jones.

Children:

2.2011 i.   + Ludlow Jones
2.2012 ii.   Charlesetta Jones   (1844)
2.2013 iii.   Josephine Jones   (c. 1846-1871)
2.2014 iv.   Charles Allibone Jones, Jr.   (1849-1850)

2.2011 Ludlow 4 Jones* *(Charlotte3 James2 Israel1)*
        b. 1844 May 04, Cincinnati, OH
        d. 1924 May 23, Springfield, OH
        bur: Spring Grove Cemetery, Cincinnati, OH (Section-23 Lot-95)

*He changed his surname to ApJones, 1879. Attended Harvard University and Cincinnati Law School; member of the Masonic Club of Springfield, Ohio; member of the Federated Church, Atascadero, CA.[lxxiv] He traveled extensively throughout Europe and Asia, and "acquired 25,000 square square miles on the mainland of Borneo and some of the islands of the Philippines, intending to sell to the United States a naval station at Ambong Bay. He could not live in the Tropics and gave up the project."[lxxv]

        m. Anna Swenson, 1875 Jun 25, Wood Lake, WI
        b. 1853 Feb 18, Christiana, Norway
        d. 1910 Jul 31, Springfield, OH
        bur: Spring Grove Cemetery, Cincinnati, OH (Section-23 Lot-95)

Children:

2.3018 i   + Eleanor Ludlow Jones

2.3018 Eleanor Ludlow "Nellie" 5 Jones *(Ludlow4 Charlotte3 James2 Israel1)*
        b. 1876 Aug 09, Chicago, IL
        d. 1968 Jan 17, Springfield, OH
        bur: Pleasant Hill Cemetery, New Moorefield, OH

m. Frank Eipper, 1901 Nov 27, Tremont Co., OH
b. 1872 Jan 17, Terre Haute, OH
d. 1954 Jan 29, Mechanicsburg, OH
bur: Pleasant Hill Cemetery, New Moorefield, OH

Son of Henry and Christena (Shuirr) Eipper.

Children:

2.4029 i.		Sarah Bella Eipper	(1902-1958)
2.4030 ii.		Anna Eipper	(1905-1978)
2.4031 iii.		Frank Ludlow Eipper	(1907-1990)
2.4032 iv.	+	Eleanor Eipper	
2.4033 v.	+	Charles Eipper	
2.4034 vi.		Josephine Eipper	(1916-1917)
2.4035 vii.	+	Florence Louise Eipper	

2.4032 Eleanor 6 Eipper *(Eleanor5 Ludlow4 Charlotte3 James2 Israel1)*
b. 1910 Sep 09, Springfield, OH
d. 2006 Mar 05, Springfield, OH
bur: unk

m. Leroy Dwayne Carpenter, 1934 Oct 31, Richmond, IN
b. 1901 Nov 07, Springfield, OH
d. 1977 Jul 21, Springfield, OH
bur: unk

Son of Charles and Mary Ann (Mount) Carpenter.

Children:

2.5082 i.	+	Don Leroy Carpenter
2.5083 ii.	+	Emily Ilene Carpenter

2.5082 Don Leroy 7 Carpenter *(Eleanor6 Eleanor5 Ludlow4 Charlotte3 James2 Israel1)*
b. 1947 Mar 03, Springfield, OH

m. Junko Kusuhara, 1968 Oct 26, Los Angeles, CA

Children:

2.6127 i.   David Carpenter

2.5083 Emily Ilene 7 Carpenter *(Eleanor6 Eleanor5 Ludlow4 Charlotte3 James2 Israel1)*
  b. 1948, OH

  m1 Ralph E. Phillips, 1968 Apr 05, Springfield, OH
  m2 Jerry L. Fender, 1972, Tampa, FL
  m3 Robert Eugene Culver, 1982 Jun 18, Tampa, FL

Children(m3):

2.6128 i.   Brian Keith Culver

2.4033 Charles 6 Eipper *(Eleanor5 Ludlow4 Charlotte3 James2 Israel1)*
  b. 1913 Mar 11, Springfield, OH
  d. 1993 Oct 20, Springfield, OH
  bur: Pleasant Hill Cemetery, New Moorefield, OH

  m. Marjorie Elizabeth Booher, 1943 May 19, Northridge, OH
  b. 1918 Sep 29, Dayton, OH
  d. 2002 Aug 11, Fresno, CA[lxxvi]
  bur: Pleasant Hill Cemetery, New Moorefield, OH

Children: @-adopted

2.5084 i. @   Sue Elizabeth Eipper
2.5085 ii. @   Nancy Ruth Eipper

2.4035 Florence Louise 6 Eipper *(Eleanor5 Ludlow4 Charlotte3 James2 Israel1)*
  b. 1918 Mar 14, Springfield, OH
  d. 2004 Apr 01, Ashton, IL[lxxvii]
  bur: unk

  m. Paul Richard Stout, 1941 May 10, Evanston, IL
  b. 1918 Nov 21, Hamilton, OH
  d. 2010 Dec 26, Grand Rapids, MI[lxxviii]
  bur: unk

  Son of Percy Ray Stout and Isabel (Galloway) Stout.

Children:

2.5086 i.   Linda Susan Stout   (1946-1952)
2.5087 ii. + Holly Karen Stout
2.5088 iii. + Steven Raymond Stout
2.5089 iv. + Robert Girard Stout

2.5087 Holly Karen 7 Stout *(Florence8 Eleanor5 Ludlow4 Charlotte3 James2 Israel1)*
  b. 1954 Dec 31, Elmhurst, IL

   m. Gregory Frank Accardi, 1980 Aug 10, Des Plaines, IL
   b. 1952 Nov 02, Chicago, IL

   Son of John L. and Angela (Bitetto) Accardi.

Children:

2.6129 i.	John Paul Accardi	b. 1981, IL
2.6130 ii.	Nicholas Anthony Accardi	b. 1983, IL
2.6131 iii.	Gregory Frank Accardi, Jr.	b. 1986, IL

2.5088 Steven Raymond 6 Stout *(Eleanor5 Ludlow4 Charlotte3 James2 Israel1)*
  b. 1956, IL

   m. Suzanne Marie Lutz, 1975 Nov 19, Muskegon, MI
   b. 1957

Children:

| 2.6132 i. | Pamela Marie Stout |
| 2.6133 ii. | Scott Thomas Stout |

2.5089 Robert Girard 6 Stout *(Eleanor5 Ludlow4 Charlotte3 James2 Israel1)*
  b. 1958 Apr 29, Elmhurst, IL

   m. Christine -----

2.1004 Catharine 3 Ludlow *(James2 Israel1)*
  b. 1828, Ludlow Station, OH
  d. 1905 Jan 23, Pass Christian, MS
  bur: Spring Grove Cemetery, Cincinnati, OH (Section-23 Lot-43)

   m1 John Baker, ca. 1849

   m2 Lewis Whiteman, ca. 1852
   b. 1796 Mar 23, Mason Co., KY
   d. 1861 Feb 16, Hamilton Co., OH
   bur: Spring Grove Cemetery, Cincinnati, OH (Section-30 Lot-15)

   Son of Benjamin Whiteman and Catherine (Davis) Whiteman.

2.1005 Benjamin Chambers 3 Ludlow *(James2 Israel1)*

    b. 1832, "Ludlow Station", OH
    d. 1898 Jan 10, Los Angeles, CA[lxxix]
    bur: Rosedale Cemetery, Los Angeles, CA (Section-N Lot-215)

Educated at Cary's College, Cincinnati, Ohio; Kenyon College, Gambier, Ohio; University of Pennsylvania, Philadelphia, graduated 1854; Cincinnati physician. Brevet Brigadier General of the Civil War. Appointed Captain of "Fremont's Hussars". Served as aide on staff of Major General Hooker at Chancellorsville. Served under Major General Meade at Gettysburg and Williamstown. In 1862, he was promoted to Major, and in 1863 he achieved the rank of Lieutenant Colonel.

    m. Frances Jones
    b. 1849 Dec --, Cincinnati, OH
    d. 1936 Apr 25, Mineola, NY[lxxx]
    bur: Melville Cemetery, Melville, NY (Section-D Lot-84)

Children:

2.2015	i.	+	Israel Ludlow
2.2016	ii.	+	Randell Hunt Ludlow
2.2017	iii.	+	Ethel C. Ludlow
2.2018	iv.	+	Charles A. Ludlow
2.2019	v.	+	Frances Ludlow

2.2015 Israel 4 Ludlow *(Benjamin3 James2 Israel1)*

    b. 1873 Apr --, Austin, TX
    d. 1955, NY
    bur: Melville Cemetery, Melville, NY (Section-D Lot-84)

A pioneer in aviation, he was referred to as the "inventor of the aeroplane" in some early newspaper accounts. In April of 1906, while piloting his plane at Atlantic Beach, Florida, he "ascended to a height of 150 or 200 feet, where he encountered a strong cross-wind." The plane plunged to the ground and newspapers from coast-to-coast relayed the news of his "fatal" injuries.[lxxxi] Ludlow recovered, although paralyzed, and lived almost another 50 years.

2.2016 Randell Hunt 4 Ludlow *(Benjamin3 James2 Israel1)*

    b. 1875 Apr --, Austin, TX
    d. 1908 May 03, Plainville, NJ[lxxxii]
    bur: Spring Grove Cemetery, Cincinnati, OH (Section-23 Lot-43)

2.2017 Ethel C. ₄ Ludlow *(Benjamin3 James2 Israel1)*

    b. 1876 Aug –, Austin, TX
    d. 1943 Nov 20, Mineola, NY
    bur: unk

2.2018 Charles Allibone ₄ Ludlow *(Benjamin3 James2 Israel1)*

    b. 1879 Feb 20, Austin, TX
    d. 1966 Feb 15, Brooklyn, NY
    bur: unk

    m. Marguerite VanTuyl Hall, 1905 Oct 04, New York, NY[lxxxiii]
    b. 1877 Nov 21, Brockville, Ontario, Canada[lxxxiv]
    d. 1971 Jul 05, Brooklyn, NY
    bur: unk

Children:

2.3019 i.   Muriel Ludlow   b. 1923, NY

2.2019 Frances "Fanny" ₄ Ludlow *(Benjamin3 James2 Israel1)*

    b. 1883 Mar 16, Austin, TX
    d. 1975 Mar 03, West Palm Beach, FL
    bur: Woodlawn Cemetery, Palm Beach, FL (Block-25A Lot-5)

2.1006 Ruhamah "Ammie" ₃ Ludlow *(James2 Israel1)*

    b. 1833 Aug 17, "Ludlow Station", OH
    d. 1913 May 17, Paterson, NJ[lxxxv]
    bur: Spring Grove Cemetery, Cincinnati, OH (Section-23 Lot-42)

"She was one of the originators of the National Audobon Society and of the national body of the Humane Society." After her marriage in 1854, she moved from Cincinnati to reside in New Orleans, Louisiana. In 1892, she moved to Indianapolis, Indiana, to reside with her niece, Mrs. Benedict.
She was visiting friends and relatives in New Jersey at the time of her death.

    m. Randell Hunt, 1854 Jul 12, Cincinnati, OH[lxxxvi]
    b. 1806 Dec 31, Charleston, SC
    d. 1892 Mar 22, New Orleans, LA
    bur: Metairie Cemetery, New Orleans, LA

    Son of Thomas and Louisa (Gaillard) Hunt. Elected to the Louisiana House of Representatives, 1840 and 1842; Professor of Law at University of Louisiana (Tulane). Hunt was elected to the United States Senate in 1866.[lxxxvii]

2.1008 Israel 3 Ludlow (James2 Israel1)

       b. 1841, "Ludlow Station", OH
       d. 1873 Apr 28, Fredericksburg, TX[lxxxviii]
       bur: Spring Grove Cemetery, Cincinnati, OH (Section-23 Lot-42)

Educated at Andover, Massachusetts, and Yellow Springs, Ohio. During the Civil War he was with the 5th United States Artillery, participating in the battles of Shiloh, Perryville, Dogwalk, Stone River and Chickamauga. It was at Chickamauga that he was wounded and captured, being afterward confined to Libby Prison. After his exchange, he was in the battle of Cold Harbor and at Petersburg during the final engagements of the war.

Following the Civil War, he studied law and began practice in Cincinnati, however, due to his failing health, he removed to Texas, where he died in 1873. [lxxxix]

Sarah Bella Dunlop Ludlow
and Salmon P. Chase
Photo courtesy of Frank Hoyt Moore

Salmon P. Chase and daughters
Janet "Nettie" (left) and Kate (right)
Photo courtesy of Frank Hoyt Moore

Nettie Chase and William Sprague Hoyt
Jeannette Jeffery Sweet Collection, courtesy of Shar Dahl

Franklin Chase Hoyt
Photo courtesy of Frank Hoyt Moore

Janet Ralston Chase
Photo courtesy of Frank Hoyt Moore

"Susie and Sammy Ludlow (9 mo.)"
Susan Middlecoff Ludlow and Samuel F. Ludlow
Jeannette Jeffery Sweet Collection, courtesy of Shar Dahl

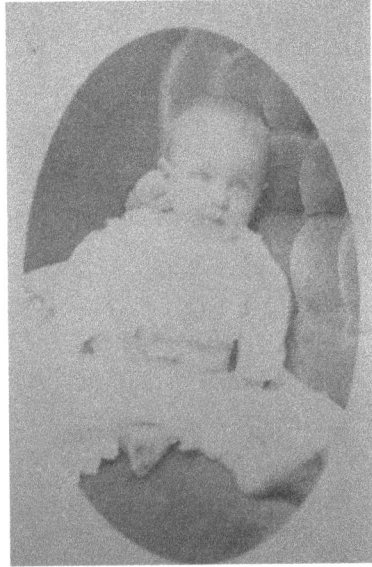

"Randell Ludlow 1 yr. + 1 mo."
Randell, son of Benjamin C. Ludlow
Jeannette Jeffery Sweet Collection, courtesy of Shar Dahl

"Susan Middlecoff and James Dunlop Ludlow,
Cincinnati, Ohio"
Jeannette Jeffery Sweet Collection, courtesy of Shar Dahl

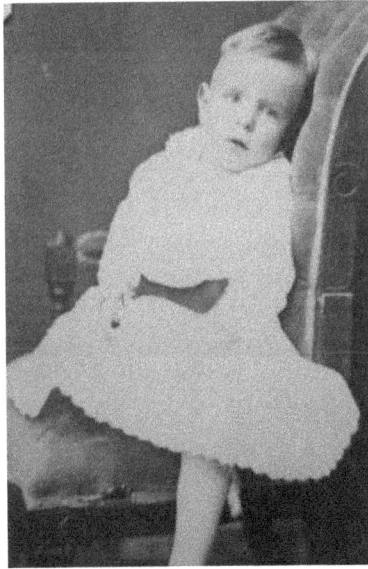

"Israel Ludlow 2 yr. + 1 mo."
Israel, son of Benjamin C. Ludlow
Jeannette Jeffery Sweet Collection, courtesy of Shar Dahl

Susan Middlecoff Ludlow
Jeannette Jeffery Sweet Collection, courtesy of Shar Dahl

Ethel C. Ludlow, 1876-1943

Jeannette Jeffery Sweet Collection, courtesy of Shar Dahl

(Photo, above) Gen. Benjamin C. Ludlow, 1831-1898, seated at left
(gentleman at right unknown)
Jeannette Jeffery Sweet Collection, courtesy of Shar Dahl

(Photo, opposite page)-Israel Ludlow, son of Benjamin Chambers Ludlow, seated at right
(gentleman standing at left unknown)
Jeannette Jeffery Sweet Collection, courtesy of Shar Dahl

Dorothy and Theresa White, Paxton, Illinois, Christmas 1902

Jeannette Jeffery Sweet Collection, courtesy of Shar Dahl

Top row, far left, Katherine Ludlow White; middle, Theresa Ludlow Benedict;
Bottom row, far left, Samuel Ludlow.
Paxton, Illinois, 1902

Jeannette Jeffery Sweet Collection, courtesy of Shar Dahl

Standing, L-R: William O. Jeffery III, Katherine Ludlow White, Cedric C. & Katherine White Gifford.
On Couch, L-R: Theresa White Jeffery, Helen Ludlow Messenger, Sam Ludlow
On Floor, L-R: Charlotte White, Adele Messenger, Jeannette Jeffery
Jeannette Jeffery Sweet Collection, courtesy of Shar Dahl

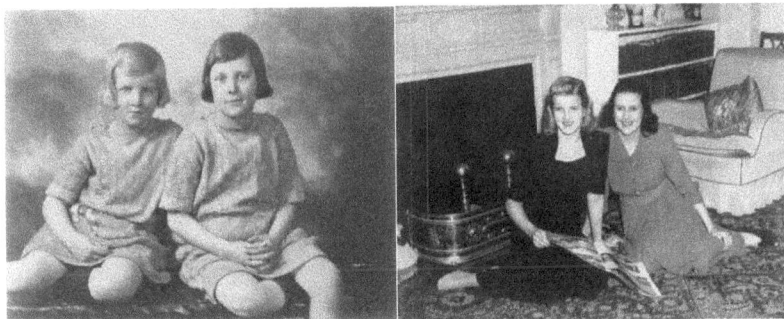

Above, sisters Beatrix Chase Hoyt (left) and (right) Constance Maud Hoyt,
daughters of
Franklin Chase Hoyt
(ca. 1922, left; ca. 1938, right)
Photo courtesy of Frank Hoyt Moore

77

The Martha Catherine Ludlow Dudley family plot.
The graves are all unmarked, except that of her grandmother,
Catherine Hamilton Chambers, whose monument is at left.

Spring Grove Cemetery
Section 35 Lot 178

Martha Catharine Ludlow

3.0001 Martha Catherine 2 Ludlow *(Israel1)*
>   b. 1799 Oct 09, Ludlow Station, OH
>   d. 1834 Oct 17, Cincinnati, OH[xc]
>   bur: Spring Grove Cemetery, Cincinnati, OH (Section-35 Lot-178)

Of the four children of Col. Israel Ludlow, the life of Martha Catharine Ludlow remains the greatest mystery. We do know that the name given to her was to honor both of her grandmothers...Martha Lyon Ludlow on her paternal side and Catharine Hamilton Chambers on her maternal side. In the years immediately following Col. Ludlow's death, Charlotte Ludlow and her children lived in Cincinnati, although the daughters were sent elsewhere for their formal education.[xci] When Martha Catharine married in 1816, her husband was ten years her senior and a member of a notable Lexington, Kentucky, family. They resided in Lexington until about 1828, when they moved to Cincinnati.[xcii] In 1834, a wave of cholera swept through Cincinnati, and Martha Catharine Ludlow Dudley fell victim to the deadly disease. Originally buried in Cincinnati's Presbyterian churchyard, her remains were moved to Spring Grove Cemetery in 1852.

>   m. Ambrose Simeon Dudley, 1816 Nov 13, Cincinnati, OH
>   b. 1789 Jan 27, Lexington, KY
>   d. 1875 May 01, Paxton, IL[xciii]
>   bur: Glen Cemetery, Paxton, IL

    Son of Rev. Ambrose and Ann (Parker) Dudley. "He was made Colonel of a Regiment under General William Henry Harrison, and took an active part in the War of 1812. He here formed the acquaintance and friendship of Gen. Harrison, and during this campaign was present and took part in the famous Battle of the Thames, fought Oct. 5, 1813, and stood over the dead body of the renowned chief, Tecumseh, who fell at that time, and whose name was so well known in the annals of those early days." [xciv]

Children:

3.1001 i.   + Ethelburt Ludlow Dudley
3.1002 ii.   + Louise Dudley
3.1003 iii. + Charlotte A. Dudley
3.1004 iv.   + Ellen Catherine Dudley

3.1001 Ethelburt Ludlow 3 Dudley *(Martha 2 Israel 1)*
    b. 1818 Feb 25, Lexington, KY
    d. 1862 Feb 20, Columbia, KY
    bur: Lexington Cemetery, Lexington, KY (Section-O Lot-147)

Educated at Harvard University and graduated from Transylvania Medical College. He was a member of Transylvania's faculty at and a prominent Lexington physician. During the Civil War, he was Colonel of the 21st Regiment, Kentucky Volunteers and died of typhoid at Columbia, Kentucky.

    m. Mary Dewees Scott, 1843 Apr 04
    b. 1817 Jul 21, Lexington, KY
    d. 1902 Feb 24, Washington, DC[xcv]
    bur: Lexington Cemetery, Lexington, KY (Section-O Lot-147)

Children:

3.2001	i.	Matthew Scott Dudley	(1844-1866)
3.2002	ii. +	Louise Ludlow Dudley	

3.2002 Louise Ludlow 4 Dudley *(Ethelburt 3 Martha 2 Israel 1)*
    b. 1849 Feb 20, Lexington, KY
    d. 1911 Sep 19, North Hatley, Quebec, Canada[xcvi]
    bur: Lexington Cemetery, Lexington, KY (Section-O Lot-151)

    m. Joseph Cabell Breckinridge, 1868 Jul 21, Lexington, KY
    b. 1842 Jan 14, Baltimore, MD
    d. 1920 Aug 18, Washington, DC[xcvii]
    bur: Lexington Cemetery, Lexington, KY (Section-O Lot-151)

Son of Rev. Robert J. Breckinridge and Anne (Preston) Breckinridge. In 1861, he joined the Union Army serving at the battlefields of Shiloh and Mill Springs. Captured by Confederate forces, he was afterward exchanged, serving during the remainder of the war as a mustering officer and receiving several promotions. In 1889, Breckinridge was promoted to brigadier general and Inspector General of the Army; followed by a promotion to Major General of volunteers in the Spanish-American War.
"In the Santiago campaign, July 2, 1898, his horse was shot from under him; he was in command of 45,000 men at Camp George H. Thomas, at Chickamauga Park, Georgia, August 1898; and he was inspector-general for fifteen years." He served also as "president-general of the Society of the Sons of the Revolution....and a member of many patriotic societies."[xcviii]

Children:

3.3001	i.	+	Mary Dudley Breckinridge	
3.3002	ii.		Robert Jefferson Breckinridge	(1870-1871)
3.3003	iii.	+	Joseph Cabell Breckinridge, Jr.	
3.3004	iv.		Louise Dudley Breckinridge	(1873-1874)
3.3005	v.	+	Ethelburt Ludlow Dudley Breckinridge	
3.3006	vi.		Mabell Warfield Breckinridge	(1877-1878)
3.3007	vii.	+	Lucian Scott Breckinridge	
3.3008	viii.	+	Lucy Hayes Breckinridge	
3.3009	ix.	+	Scott Dudley Breckinridge	
3.3010	x.		Charles Henry Preston Breckinridge	(1884-1885)
3.3011	xi.	+	Henry Skillman Breckinridge	
3.3012	xii.	+	Margaret Scott Skillman Breckinridge	
3.3013	xiii.	+	John Preston Breckinridge	

3.3001 Mary Dudley 5 Breckinridge *(Louise4 Ethelburt3 Martha2 Israel1)*

> b. 1869 Jul 20, San Francisco, CA
> d. 1939 Sep 09, Daylesford, PA
> bur: Arlington National Cemetery, Arlington, VA (Section-6 site-8594)

> m. John Fore Hines, 1898 Oct 19, Lexington, KY
> b. 1870 Sep 22, Bowling Green, KY
> d. 1941 Oct 19, Daylesford, PA[xcix]
> bur: Arlington National Cemetery, Arlington, VA (Section-6 site-8594)

Son of Henry Clay Hines and Sally (Fore) Hines. He graduated from the U.S. Naval Academy in 1892 and the US Naval College in 1910. He served on the USS Dorothea during the Spanish-American War. He also served on the cruiser Cincinnati, 1905-1907. Executive officer of the battleship North Carolina, 1910-1912. In 1917, he was promoted to the rank of Captain and commanded four cruisers. Received both the Navy Cross and the Distinguished Service Medal.[c]

Children:

3.4001	i.		Joseph Cabell Breckinridge Hines	(1901)
3.4002	ii.	+	Louise Dudley Hines	
3.4003	iii.	+	John Fore Hines, Jr.	
3.4004	iv.	+	Mary Breckinridge Hines	

3.4002 Louise Dudley 6 Hines *(Mary5 Louise4 Ethelburt3 Martha2 Israel1)*
      b. 1903 Jul 24, Annapolis, MD
      d. 1996 Apr 25, Devon, PA
    bur: St. Peter's Church in the Great Valley, Malvern, PA

      m. George Bryan Kneass, 1923 Jun 09, Philadelphia, PA (div. 1951)
      b. 1897 Oct 25, Philadelphia, PA
      d. 1972 May--, Bryn Mawr, PA
      bur: Gladwyne, PA

Son of Strickland Landis Kneass and Mary Stewart (Edwards) Kneass.
He graduated from the University of Pennsylvania in 1918. He served as a USN aviator during WWI and as U.S. Assistant Secretary of the Treasury under President Dwight D. Eisenhower.

Children:

3.5001 i.   +   Mary Stewart Edwards Kneass
3.5002 ii.   +   George Bryan Kneass, Jr.

3.5001 Mary Stewart Edwards "Polly" 6 Kneass *(Mary5 Louise4 Etthelburt3 Martha2 Israel1)*
      b. 1925 May 26, Philadelphia, PA
      d. 2000 Feb 29, Red Bank, NJ
    bur: St. Peter's Church in the Great Valley, Malvern, PA

      m. Emmett Edward Kelly, 1945 Aug 11, Ventura, CA
      b. 1919 Apr 03, Bassett, AR
      d. 1989 Jan 14, Red Bank, NJ
      bur: c

Son of Eugene Kelly and Ora Belle (Kyle) Kelly. He graduated from Southwestern College [Rhodes College], Memphis, TN. Joined the US Navy in 1942 and was stationed in the Admiralty Islands.
He was honorably discharged from the Navy in 1946 with the rank of Lieutenant.

Children:

3.6001 i.   +   Louise Dudley Kelly
3.6002 ii.   +   Charles Edward Kelly
3.6003 iii.   +   Stewart Emmett Kelly
3.6004 iv.   +   John Bryan Kelly

3.6001 Louise Dudley 6 Kelly *(Mary5 Louise4 Ethelburt3 Martha2 Israel1)*
         b. 1952, NY

3.6002 Charles Edward 6 Kelly *(Mary5 Louise4 Ethelburt3 Martha2 Israel1)*
         b. 1954, NY

         m. Amy Landers, 1983, Chattanooga, TN

Children:

3.7001	i.	Meaghan Landers Kelly	b. 1989
3.7002	ii.	Shannon Breckinridge Kelly	b. 1990
3.7003	iii.	Mary Cabell Kelly	b. 1993

3.6003 Stewart Emmett 6 Kelly *(Mary5 Louise4 Ethelburt3 Martha2 Israel1)*
         b. 1955, NY

         m. Leila Jane Berry, 1978, Scottsville, KY
         b. 1957, KY

Children:

| 3.7004 | i. | Anne Warfield Kelly |
| 3.7005 | ii. | Kathryn Ashe Kelly |

3.6004 John Bryan 6 Kelly *(Mary5 Louise4 Ethelburt3 Martha2 Israel1)*
         b. 1958, NJ

3.5002 George Bryan "GB" 6 Kneass, Jr. *(Mary5 Louise4 Ethelburt3 Martha2 Israel1)*
         b. 1926 Oct 02, Bryn Mawr, PA
         d. 1990 Feb 24, Bryn Mawr, PA
         bur: St. David's Cemetery, Wayne, PA

Attended Williams College. He loved being outdoors; playing squash and tennis; and was the vice-president for a lithium mining company.[ci]

         m. Anita (Wood) Clement, 1956 Sep 09, Bryn Mawr, PA
         b. 1929 Sep 02, Philadelphia, PA

Widow of Dewitt C. Clement. The children from her first marriage were adopted by their step-father, George B. Kneass.*[cii]

Children: @-adopted stepchildren

3.6005 i. @ + Dewitt Clement Kneass
3.6006 ii. @ + Anita Wood Kneass
3.6007 iii. + Susan Breckinridge Kneass
3.6008 iv. + Strickland Landis Kneass

3.6005 Dewitt Clement Kneass
       b. 1952, PA

       m. Glory Czerniak

3.6006 Anita Clement Kneass
       b. 1953, PA

       m. Tim Conner

Children:

3.7006 i.   Ashley Kneass Conner
3.7007 ii.   Margaret Breckinridge Conner

3.6007 Susan Breckinridge 7 Kneass *(George6 Mary5 Louise4 Ethelburt3 Martha2 Israel1)*
       b. 1957, NH

       m. Keith George Laursen, 1986 Jul 12, St. David's, Wayne, PA
       b. 1961, NJ

       Son of George Keith Laursen and Mary (Grasso).

Children:

3.7008 i.   Kevin Bryan Laursen   b. 1989, CT
3.7009 ii.   Kelsey Anita Laursen   b. 1993, CT

3.6008 Strickland Landis 7 Kneass *(George6 Mary5 Louise4 Ethelburt3 Martha2 Israel1)*
       b. 1960, TN

3.4003 John Fore 6 Hines, Jr. *(Mary5 Louise4 Ethelburt3 Martha2 Israel1)*
  b. 1906 Jan 18, Manila, Philippines
  d. 1982 May 12, Devon, PA
  bur: US Naval Academy Cemetery, Annapolis, MD (Section-6 Lot-1183)

Graduated from the US Naval Academy, 1927. During WWII he served on the
aircraft carrier Lexington. He received the Bronze Star for his duty as gunnery
officer aboard the USS San Juan. Also received a Commendation Medal for
meritorious service as executive officer aboard the USS Oklahoma City.
He retired in 1948 with the rank of Rear Admiral. He subsequently served on
the staff of American International College as president, 1955-1970.

  m. Mary Janet Earle, 1929 May 11, Worcester, MA
  b. 1906 Jul 22, Wyncote, PA
  d. 1981 Feb 19, Annapolis, MD
  bur: US Naval Academy Cemetery, Annapolis, MD (Section-6 Lot-1183)

Children

3.5003 i. + John Fore Hines III
3.5004 ii. + Ralph Earle Hines

3.5003 John Fore 7 Hines III *(John6 Mary5 Louise4 Ethelburt3 Martha2 Israel1)*
  b. 1935, MA

3.5004 Ralph Earle 7 Hines *(John6 Mary5 Louise4 Ethelburt3 Martha2 Israel1)*
  b. 1938 May 26, Springfield, MA
  d. 1967 Feb 19, Thua Thien-Hu, South Vietnam
  bur: Arlington National Cemetery, Arlington, VA (Section-6 site-5789)

"Posthumously awarded the Bronze Star for meritorious achievement. When a
platoon of his company successfully ambushed an enemy unit, Captain Hines
personally moved to the scene of action, inflicted heavy casualties on the
enemy and captured the enemy commander. He continued to lead his men in
an exemplary manner until the 19th of February, 1967, when he fell, mortally
wounded by an enemy land mine. By his outstanding courage, leadership and
unyielding devotion to duty, Captain Hines served as to inspire all who
observed him and upheld the highest traditions of the Marine Corps and the
United States Naval Service. He gallantly gave his life for his country".[ciii]

  m. Elizabeth Perry Sudmeyer

Children:

3.6009 i.   Scott Breckinridge Hines

3.4004 Mary Breckinridge 6 Hines *(Mary5 Louise4 Ethelburt3 Martha2 Israel1)*
        b. 1909 Jul 20, Annapolis, MD
        d. 2005 June 8, Devon, PA[civ]
        bur: West Laurel Cemetery, Bala Cynwyd, PA (Section-Moreland L-314)

        m. Edward Blanchard Hodge, Jr., 1934 May 05, Philadelphia, PA[cv]
        b. 1906 May 23, Philadelphia, PA
        d. 1981 Oct 17, Waterloo Mills, PA
        bur: West Laurel Cemetery, Bala Cynwyd, PA (Section-Moreland L-314)

        Son of Edward B. Hodge, Sr. and Gretchen (Green) Hodge. Graduated, 1928, Princeton University; University of Pennsylvania Law School, 1931.

Children:

3.5005 i.   +   Edward Blanchard Hodge III
3.5006 ii.   +   John Hines Hodge

3.5005 Edward Blanchard 7 Hodge III *(Mary6 Mary5 Louise4 Ethelburt3 Martha2 Israel1)*
        b. 1941

        m. Judith Schwartz, 1968

Children:

3.6010 i.   Edward Blanchard Hodge IV
3.6011 ii.   William Hodge

3.5006 John Hines 7 Hodge *(Mary6 Mary5 Louise4 Ethelburt3 Martha2 Israel1)*
        b. 1944

        m. Mary Elizabeth Gindhart, 1973 Mar 03, Trenton, NJ[cvi]

Children:

3.6012 i.   John Cortlandt Hodge
3.6013 ii.   Joseph Cabell Hodge

3.3003 Joseph Cabell 5 Breckinridge, Jr. *(Louise4 Ethelburt3 Martha2 Israel1)*

> b. 1872 Mar 06, Ft. Monroe, VA
> d. 1898 Feb 11, near Havana, Cuba
> bur: Lexington Cemetery, Lexington, KY

Swept overboard from the torpedo boat "Cushing" while carrying dispatches to the battleship "Maine", and drowned.

3.3005 Ethelburt Ludlow Dudley 5 Breckinridge *(Louise4 Ethelburt3 Martha2 Israel1)*

> b. 1875 Jul 17, Lexington, KY
> d. 1914 Jul 26, Asheville, NC[cvii]
> bur: Lexington Cemetery, Lexington, KY (Section-O Lot-147)

Captain, US Infantry, served during the Spanish-American War.

> m. Genevieve Pearson Mattingly, 1899 Apr 04
> b. 1878 Jul 12, Washington, DC
> d. 1957 Mar 20, Lexington, KY[cviii]
> bur: Lexington Cemetery, Lexington, KY (Section-O Lot-147)

Children:

3.4005	i.	+	Joseph Cabell Breckinridge III
3.4006	ii.	+	William Mattingly Breckinridge
3.4007	iii.	+	Genevieve Dudley Breckinridge
3.4008	iv.	+	Ethelburt Ludlow Dudley Breckinridge, Jr.

3.4005 Joseph Cabell 6 Breckinridge III *(Ethelburt5 Louise4 Ethelburt3 Martha2 Israel1)*

> b. 1900 Feb 28, Washington, DC
> d. 1971 May 16, Lexington, KY[cix]
> bur: Lexington Cemetery, Lexington, KY (Section-O Lot-147)

Graduated Culver Military Academy, 1920. He attained the rank of colonel during WWII, serving afterward with the War Crimes Commission in Europe.

> m. Marie Reine "Renee" Fusz, 1929
> b. 1905 Dec 25, MO
> d. 1955 May 24, Lexington, KY[cx]
> bur: Lexington Cemetery, Lexington, KY (Section-O Lot-147)

Children:

3.5007	i.	+	Joan Cabell Breckinridge

3.5007 Joan Cabell 7 Breckinridge *(Joseph6 Ethelburt5 Louise4 Ethelburt3 Martha2 Israel1)*
   b. 1941 Apr 28, Lexington, KY
   d. 2000 Dec 06, Lexington, KY
   bur: Lexington Cemetery, Lexington, KY (Section-O Lot-146)

3.4006 William Mattingly 6 Breckinridge *(Ethelburt5 Louise4 Ethelburt3 Martha2 Israel1)*
   b. 1905 Nov 06, Washington, DC
   d. 1996 May 01, Valley Head, WV
   bur: Arlington National Cemetery, Arlington, VA (Section-N court-2)

   Received Distinguished Service Medal and the Legion of Merit. He achieved the rank of Major General.

   m. Lillian Frances Naylor, 1928
   b. 1906 Mar 13, Stephenville, TX
   d. 1987 May 05, Sarasota, FL
   bur: Arlington National Cemetery, Arlington, VA (Section-N court-2)

Children:

3.5008 i.   +   Barbara Breckinridge

3.5008 Barbara 7 Breckinridge *(William6 Ethelburt5 Louise4 Ethelburt3 Martha2 Israel1)*
   b. 1935, Panama

3.4007 Genevieve Dudley 6 Breckinridge *(Ethelburt5 Louise4 Ethelburt3 Martha2 Israel1)*
   b. 1912 Jul 23, Ancon, Canal Zone, Panama
   d. 1999 Feb 09, Randolph Co. WV
   bur: Mountain View Cemetery, Charleston, WV

   m. Neil Robinson II, 1936 Apr 18, Lexington, KY[cxi]
   b. 1913 Jun 29, Charleston, WV
   d. 1974 Mar 10, Charleston, WV[cxii]
   bur: Mountain View Cemetery, Charleston, WV

   Son of Carel and Caroline (Roller) Robinson. Graduate of Lehigh University. Mining Engineer and president of Robinson & Robinson, Inc. Member of the American Institute of Mining, Metallurgical, and Petroleum Engineers; Association of Iron and Steel Engineers; West Virginia and National Society of Professional Engineers; Interstate Coal Conference; the Metropolitan Club of New York.

Children:

3.5009 i.   +   Dudley Breckinridge Robinson
3.5010 ii.   +   Caroline Roller Robinson
3.5011 iii.   Genevieve Pearson Mattingly Robinson (1942-1960)
3.5012 iv.   +   Margaret Maury Robinson
3.5013 v.   +   Lucy Hayes Robinson

3.5009 Dudley Breckinridge 7 Robinson *(Genevieve6 Ethelburt5 Louise4 Ethelburt3 Martha 2 Israel1)*
        b. 1938

        m1 George Eisele Fisher, Jr., 1958 Nov 15, Charleston,, WV
        b. 1931 Sep 08, NJ
        d. 1985 Jan 04, Hampton, VA
        bur: Grace Episcopal Churchyard, Yorktown, VA

        Son of George Eisele Fisher, Sr. and Jane (Jorphy) Fisher.

        m2 Ronald Angus McKenney, 1989 Apr 08, Charleston, WV
        b. 1937 Apr 15, Alexandria, VA
        d. 2008 Nov 22, Beaufort, SC
        bur: St. Helena's Episcopal Churchyard, Beaufort, SC

        Son of Alvin McKenney and Hazel (Webber) McKenney.

Children(m1):

3.6014 i.   +   George Eisele Fisher III
3.6015 ii.   +   Neil Robinson Fisher
3.6016 iii. +   Edwin Adam Fisher
3.6017 iv.   William Mattingly Fisher

3.6014 George Eisele 8 Fisher III *(Dudley7 Genevieve6 Ethelburt5 Louise4 Ethelburt3 Martha2 Israel1)*

        m. Colleen Lyons, 1985

Children:

3.7010 i.   Catherine Hayes Fisher
3.7011 ii.   Caroline Alberton Fisher
3.7012 iii.   George Pearson Fisher

3.6015 Neil Robinson 7 Fisher *(Genevieve6 Ethelburt5 Louise4 Ethelburt3 Martha2 Israel1)*

m. Myra Cash, 1984 Sep

Children:

3.7013 i.   Neil Robinson Fisher, Jr.
3.7014 ii. Elizabeth Breckinridge Fisher
3.7015 iii. Rebecca Catherine Fisher
3.7016 iv. John Eisele Fisher

3.6016 Edwin Adam 7 Fisher *(Genevieve6 Ethelburt5 Louise4 Ethelburt3 Martha2 Israel1)*

m. Rhonda Thaxton, 1996

Children:

3.7017 i.   Emily Grace Fisher
3.7018 ii. Megan Eisele Fisher

3.5010 Caroline Roller 7 Robinson *(Genevieve6 Ethelburt5 Louise4 Ethelburt3 Martha2 Israel1)*
b. 1941 Jul 01, Lexington, KY
d. 1979 Aug 03
bur: unk

m. John Bankhead Banks, Jr., 1971 Jan 30, Charleston, WV[cxiii]
b. 1941, WV

Children:

3.6017 i.   Genevieve Pearson Mattingly Banks
3.6018 ii. Catherine Dana Banks
3.6019 iii. John Bankhead Banks III

3.5012 Margaret Maury 7 Robinson *(Genevieve6 Ethelburt5 Louise4 Ethelburt3 Martha2 Israel1)*
b. 1945, KY

m. Robert Stark Reishman, 1968 Aug 03, Charleston, WV[cxiv]
b. 1945, WV

Son of Vincent John Reishman and Dorothy Brawley (Stark) Reishman.

Children:

3.6020	i.	Margaret Roller Reishman	b. 1970, WV
3.6021	ii.	Sarah Breckinridge Reishman	b. 1974, PA
3.6022	iii.	Robert Stark Reishman, Jr.	b. 1977, PA

3.5013 Lucy Hayes 7 Robinson *(Genevieve6 Ethelburt5 Louise4 Ethelburt3 Martha2 Israel1)*

    b. 1949

    m. John William Eilers, 1976

Children:

3.6023	i.	William Robinson Eilers
3.6024	ii.	John Dudley Eilers
3.6025	iii.	Sarah Elizabeth Eilers

3.4008 Ethelburt Ludlow Dudley 6 Breckinridge, Jr. *(Ethelburt5 Louise4 Ethelburt3 Martha2 Israel1)*

    b. 1914 Aug 03, Lexington, KY
    d. 1982 Aug 13, Clarksville, TN
    bur: Lexington Cemetery, Lexington, KY (Section-O Lot-151)

Major, US Artillery during WWII; recipient, Silver Star and the Bronze Star.

    m. Susan Lewis Swinford, 1945 Jul 21, Lexington, KY
    b. 1916 May 08, Cynthiana, KY
    d. 1996 May 06, Lexington, KY
    bur: Lexington Cemetery, Lexington, KY (Section-O Lot-147)

3.3007 Lucian Scott 5 Breckinridge *(Louise4 Ethelburt3 Martha2 Israel1)*

    b. 1879 Dec 01, Washington, DC
    d. 1941 Oct 13, New York, NY[cxv]
    bur: Lexington Cemetery, Lexington, KY (Section-O Lot-151)

Served as commander of Company B, 308th Infantry, 7th Division, during WWI. Awarded the Distinguished Service Cross.

    m1 Ethel Carney, 1903 Jun 16
    b. 1877 Dec 04, Portland, ME
    d. 1904 May 12, Fort Fremont, GA[cxvi]
    bur: Lexington Cemetery, Lexington, KY (Section-O Lot-151)

m2 Elinor "Elsie" Wilkinson
b. 1879 Apr 23
d. 1952 Aug 31, New York, NY
bur: Lexington Cemetery, Lexington, KY (Section-O Lot-151)

Children(m1):

3.4009 i.   Unnamed Infant   (1904)

3.3008 Lucy Hayes 5 Breckinridge *(Louise4 Ethelburt3 Martha2 Israel1)*
> b. 1881 Jan 07, Washington, DC
> d. 1959
> bur: unk
>
> m. Henry Randolph Brigham, 1919 Jul 21, New York, NY
> b. 1880 Apr 06, Boston, MA
> d. 1964 Dec 25, Cambridge, MA[cxvii]
> bur: Mt. Auburn Cemetery, Cambridge, MA

3.3009 Scott Dudley 5 Breckinridge *(Louise4 Ethelburt3 Martha2 Israel1)*
> b. 1882 May 23, San Francisco, CA
> d. 1941 Aug 01, Lexington, KY[cxviii]
> bur: Lexington Cemetery, Lexington, KY (Section-O Lot-152)

Educated at Lafayette College; the US Military Academy and 1907 graduate of Georgetown University. An expert fencer, he was a member of the 1912 Olympic team and was twice national foil champion.

> m. Gertrude Ashby Bayne, 1911 Apr 19
> b. 1883 Oct 21, Washington, DC
> d. 1981 Feb 04, Arlington, VA
> bur: Lexington Cemetery, Lexington, KY (Section-O Lot-152)

Children:

3.4010 i.   +   John Bayne Breckinridge
3.4011 ii.   +   Scott Dudley Breckinridge, Jr.
3.4012 iii. +   Gertrude Bayne Breckinridge

3.4010 John Bayne 6 Breckinridge *(Scott5 Louise4 Ethelburt3 Martha2 Israel1)*
> b. 1913 Nov 29, Washington, DC
> d. 1979 Jul 29, Lexington, KY
> bur: Lexington Cemetery, Lexington, KY (Section-O Lot-133)

Attended schools in Lexington, Kentucky; Massie Preparatory School, Versailles, Kentucky; Tome Preparatory School, Port Deposit, Maryland; University of Kentucky, 1937. Admitted to the Kentucky Bar in 1940 and commenced the practice of law in Lexington. Served in the United States Army, 1941-1946, attaining the rank of lieutenant colonel. Served in the Kentucky House of Representatives, 1956-1960; Attorney General of Kentucky, 1960-1964; elected as Representative to United States Congress, 1973-1979.

> m1 Frances Knight Archibald, 1945 Aug 12, Broad Creek, MD (div.)
> b. 1918 Aug 24, Lexington, KY
> d. 1991 Mar 16, Austin, TX
> bur: unk
>
> m2 Helen Congleton, 1954 Jul 05, Charlottesville, VA
> b. 1916 Feb 25, Lexington, KY
> d. 2000 Aug 09, Lexington, KY
> bur: Lexington Cemetery, Lexington, KY (Section-O Lot-133)

Children(m1):

3.5014 i.   +   Frances Knight Breckinridge
3.5015 ii. +   John Bayne Breckinridge, Jr.

3.5014 Frances Knight 7 Breckinridge *(John6 Scott5 Louise4 Ethelburt3 Martha2 Israel1)*
>   b. 1946, KY
>
>   m. Stephen Osheroff, 1971 Nov 21 (div. 1998)
>   b. 1946

Children: @-adopted

3.6016 i. @   David Lucian Osheroff

3.5015 John Bayne 7 Breckinridge, Jr. *(John6 Scott5 Louise4 Ethelburt3 Martha2 Israel1)*
>   b. 1949, KY
>
>   m. Kiyoko Kiyoma, 1982 Sep 04, Jessamine Co., KY[cxix] (div.)

3.4011 Scott Dudley 6 Breckinridge, Jr. *(Scott5 Louise4 Ethelburt3 Martha2 Israel1)*
      b. 1917 Apr 17, Lexington, KY
      d. 2000 Jun 10, Lexington, KY
      bur: Lexington Cemetery, Lexington, KY (Section-O Lot-13)

"Attended the University of Kentucky, 1934-1941, earning degrees in history, political science , and law; member of the Patterson Literary Society and captain of the fencing team. He served in the Navy during WWII, patrolling the coast of Florida and in convoys in the North and South Atlantic. While on active duty, he served much of his time aboard the USS Saucy (PG-65), eventually becoming its commanding officer.

In 1953, he joined the Central Intelligence Agency, where he remained for 26 years, serving both in Washington and abroad...When he retired in 1979, he held the position of Deputy Inspector General, and had twice received the Distinguished Intelligence Medal- the CIA's highest award. [cxx]
Author of "*The CIA and the US Intelligence System*".[cxxi]

      m. Helen Virden Babbitt, 1942 Aug 29, Louisville, KY
      b. 1920, KY

3.4012 Gertrude Bayne "Trudy" 6 Breckinridge *(Scott5 Louise4 Ethelburt3 Martha2 Israel1)*
      b. 1922 Jan 20, Lexington, KY
      d. 2014 Oct 06, Charlottesville, VA
      bur: St. James Church Cemetery, Owensville, VA

      m1 Compton Sargent, 1944 Jun 24, Washington, DC
      b. 1921 Sep 24, PA
      d. 1944 Dec 23, Richland, SC
      bur: Rosedale Cemetery, Manchester-by-the-Sea, MA

      Son of Fitzwilliam Sargent and Bernice (Wellington) Sargent.

      m2 Francis Bradley Peyton III, 1948 Jan 06, Washington, DC
      b. 1917 Mar 01, Charlottesville, VA
      d. 1998 Sep 30, Charlottesville, VA
      bur: St. James Church Cemetery, Owensville, VA

      Son of William H. and Mary E. (Garth) Peyton.

Children(m2):

3.5016 i.	+	Gertrude Bayne Peyton
3.5017 ii.	+	Francis Bradley Peyton IV
3.5018 iii.	+	Scott Breckinridge Peyton

3.5016 Gertrude Bayne 7 Peyton *(Gertrude6 Scott5 Louise4 Ethelburt3 Martha2 Israel1)*
b. 1948, VA

m. Munro Cannon Russell, 1971 Apr 24, Charlottesville, VA

Children:

3.6017 i. Genevieve Bayne Russell
3.6018 ii. Munro Cannon Russell, Jr.

3.5017 Francis Bradley 7 Peyton IV *(Gertrude6 Scott5 Louise4 Ethelburt3 Martha2 Israel1)*
b. 1950, VA

m. Claudia Winant, 1974 Aug 24, Washington, DC
b. 1949, NY

Children:

3.6019 i. + Kathryn Ashby Peyton
3.6020 ii. Francis Bradley Peyton V

3.6019 Kathryn Ashby "Skye" 8 Peyton *(Francis7 Gertrude6 Scott5 Louise4 Ethelburt3 Martha2 Israel1)*
.

m. Brian Deluce

Children:

3.7019 i. Sage Deluce
3.7020 ii. Tavion Deluce

3.5018 Scott Breckinridge 7 Peyton *(Gertrude6 Scott5 Louise4 Ethelburt3 Martha2 Israel1)*
b. 1953, VA

Graduated from Virginia Polytechnic Institute and State University [Virginia Tech] in 1976 with a B.S. degree in Horticulture.

m. Margaret Page Edwards, 1980 Jan 19
b. 1952

Children:

3.6021 i. Matthew Scott Peyton   b. 1983
3.6022 ii. Stephanie Page Peyton   b. 1985

3.3011 Henry Skillman ₅ Breckinridge *(Louise4 Ethelburt3 Martha 2 Israel1)*
>   b. 1886 May 25, Chicago, IL
>   d. 1960 May 02, New York, NY
>   bur: Lexington Cemetery, Lexington, KY (Section-O Lot-152)

Attended Princeton University and Harvard Law School. He was appointed as President Woodrow Wilson's Assistant Secretary of War. He competed as a member of the 1912 US Olympic fencing team in Antwerp and was captain of the same team in 1928 in the Olympic games in Amsterdam.
He practiced law in New York where his most famous client and close friend was Col. Charles Lindbergh. During the widely-publicized trial of Bruno Hauptmann for the kidnapping of Col. Lindbergh's infant son, Breckinridge was a key witness, having been involved in the ransom negotiations.

>   m1 Ruth Woodman, 1910 Jul 09, Geneva, Switzerland (div., 1925)
>   b. 1888 Nov 17, Concord, NH
>   d. 1941 Jul 26, lost at sea
>   bur: Blossom Hill Cemetery, Concord, NH (Section-H)

On her way to London to serve as a house mother for Red Cross nurses, her ship, the SS Maasdam was torpedoed by a Nazi submarine, and she was lost at sea.[cxxii]

>   m2 Aida de Acosta Root, 1927 Aug 5 (div., 1947)
>   b. 1884 Jul 28, Elberon, NJ
>   d. 1962 May 27, Bedford, NY
>   bur: unk

She was the first woman to solo in a powered balloon (Paris, France, 1903).

>   m3 Margaret Lucy Smith, 1947 Mar 27, Carson City, NV
>   b.1913 May 31, England
>   d. 2011 Jun 10, New Paltz, NY
>   bur: Lexington Cemetery, Lexington, KY (Section-O Lot-152)

Children(m1):

3.4013 i.   + Elizabeth Foster Breckinridge
3.4014 ii.   Louise Dudley Breckinridge   (1914-1934)

Children(m3):

3.4015 iii.   Madeline Houston Breckinridge

3.4013 Elizabeth Foster 6 Breckinridge *(Henry5 Louise4 Ethelburt3 Martha2 Israel1)*
  b. 1911 Jul 10, Monterey, PA
  d. 2005 Oct 25, Washington, DC
  bur: unk

  m. John Stephens Graham, 1935 Jun 22, Washington, DC
  b. 1905 Aug 04, Reading, MA
  d. 1976 Oct 20, Washington, DC
  bur: unk

    Son of Joseph L. Graham and Margaret (Nowell) Graham.
Studied law at Harvard University and the University of Virginia. Served on the
Atomic Energy Commission and as Assistant Secretary of the US Treasury.[cxxiii]

Children:

3.5019 i.   + Louise Breckinridge Graham
3.5020 ii.   + Margaret Nowell Graham
3.5021 iii. + Katherine Foster Graham
3.5022 iv.   + Susan Perkins Graham

3.5019 Louise Breckinridge 7 Graham *(Elizabeth6 Henry5 Louise4 Ethelburt3 Martha2 Israel1)*
  b. 1937

  m1 Charles Willard Hayes III

    Son of Charles Willard Hayes, Jr. and Annie Graham (Hume) Hayes.

  m2 Raymond Barham

Children(m1):

3.6023 i.   Charles Willard Hayes IV   (1961-1993)
3.6024 ii.   + Louise Breckinridge Hayes
3.6025 iii. + Sarah Graham Hayes

3.6024 Louise Breckinridge 8 Hayes *(Louise7 Elizabeth6 Henry5 Louise4 Ethelburt3 Martha2 Israel1)*

  m. Richard David Snow

Children:

3.7021 i.   Sarah Breckinridge Snow
3.7022 ii.   Arthur Charles Snow

3.6025 Sarah Graham 8 Hayes *(Louise7 Elizabeth6 Henry5 Louise4 Ethelburt3 Martha2 Israel1)*

m. Andrew Keith Hubner

Children:

3.7023 i   Henry Hayes Hubner

3.5020 Margaret Nowell Graham
        b. 1946

m. Joseph H. Coreth

3.5021 Katherine Foster Graham

m. David Dwyer Smith

3.5022 Susan Perkins Graham
        b. 1953

m. Christopher John Bowden

Children:

3.6026 i.   Esme Eliza Bowden
3.6027 ii.   Beatrix Margaret "Trixie" Bowden
3.6028 iii.   Elizabeth Breckinridge "Lizzie" Bowden

3.3012 Margaret Scott Skillman 5 Breckinridge *(Louise4 Ethelburt3 Martha2 Israel1)*
        b. 1889 May 01, Washington, DC
        d. 1970 Jan 31, Washington, DC
        bur: Lexington Cemetery, Lexington, KY (Section-P Lot-53)

        m. John Thomas Vance, Jr., 1917, CA
        b. 1884 Aug 24, Lexington, KY
        d. 1943 Apr 13, Lexington, KY[cxxiv]
        bur: Lexington Cemetery, Lexington, KY (Section-P Lot-53)

        Son of John Thomas Vance, Sr. and Emily Chew (Gibney) Vance.

Children:

3.4016 i. + John Thomas Vance III
3.4017 ii. + Louise Ludlow Dudley Vance
3.4018 iii. + Henry Breckinridge Vance

3.4016 John Thomas 6 Vance III *(Margaret5 Louise4 Ethelburt3 Martha2 Israel1)*
        b. 1921 Oct 12, Lexington, KY
        d. 2008 Jun 15, Portland, OR[cxxv]
        bur: Missoula City Cemetery, Missoula, MT (Lot-4 Block-52)

Served in the U. S. Army during WWII; graduated from the University of Montana and George Washington University Law School. In 1968, he was appointed by President Johnson as Chairman of the Indian Claims Commission.

        m. Camilla Josephine Fox McCormick, 1946 May 26 (div. 1969)
        b. 1920 Nov 22, Missoula, MT
        d. 2005 Feb 07, Polson, MT
        bur: Missoula City Cemetery, Missoula, MT (Lot-4 Block-52)

Children:

3.5023 i. + Margaret Breckinridge Vance
3.5024 ii. + Katherine McCormick Vance
3.5025 iii. + Angela Fox Vance
3.5026 iv. + Mary Camilla Dudley Vance

3.5023 Margaret Breckinridge 7 Vance *(John6 Margaret5 Louise4 Ethelburt3 Martha2 Israel1)*
        b. 1951 Sep 19, Missoula, MT

Children:

3.6029 i. John Christopher Prescott Vance
3.6030 ii. Elizabeth Louise Kaye Vance
3.6031 iii. Isabelle Madeline Breckinridge Vance

3.5024 Katherine McCormick 7 Vance *(John6 Margaret5 Louise4 Ethelburt3 Martha2 Israel1)*
        b. 1953, OK

        m. G. Bruce Sewell

Children:

3.6032 i.   Grant Clement Sewell
3.6033 ii.   Emily Anne Sewell

3.5025 Angela Fox 7 Vance *(John6 Margaret5 Louise4 Ethelburt3 Martha2 Israel1)*
      b. 1955

      m. Paul Pendery

Children:

3.6034 i.   Kelsa Pendery
3.6035 ii.   Paul Ross Pendery

3.5026 Mary Camilla Dudley 7 Vance *(John6 Margaret5 Louise4 Ethelburt3 Martha2 Israel1)*
      b. 1925, KY

      m. Jeffrey John Strange

3.4017 Louise Ludlow Dudley 6 Vance *(Margaret5 Louise4 Ethelburt3 Martha2 Israel1)*
      b. 1925 Jan 31, Lexington, KY
      d. 1994 Jan 12, Dayton, OH
      bur: St. George's Episcopal Memorial Garden, Dayton, OH

      m. William Anderson Marsteller, 1953 Jun 12, Chevy Chase, MD
      b. 1918 Sep 16, Richmond, VA
      d. 1998 Jul 06, Dayton, OH
      bur: St. George's Episcopal Memorial Garden, Dayton, OH

Children:

3.5027 i.   + Philip William Marsteller
3.5028 ii. + Margaret Breckinridge Marsteller
3.5029 iii. + William Arell Marsteller
3.5030 iv. + Ann Cussen Marsteller

3.5027 Philip William 7 Marsteller *(Louise6 Margaret5 Louise4 Ethelburt3 Martha2 Israel1)*
      b. 1954, DC

      m. Laura Beebe, 1980 May 31, Kettering, OH

Children:

3.6036 i.   Jennifer Michelle Marsteller
3.6037 ii.   Stephanie Christine Marsteller

3.5028 Margaret Breckinridge 6 Marsteller *(Margaret5 Louise4 Ethelburt3 Martha 2 Israel1)*
        b. 1955, DC

        m. James F. Shuler, 1982 Sep 18, Oswego, NY

Children:

3.6038 i.   Carrie Ann Shuler
3.6039 ii.   Kate Shuler

3.5029 William Arell 6 Marsteller *(Margaret5 Louise4 Ethelburt3 Martha 2 Israel1)*
        b. 1957, DC

        m. Elizabeth Hintz, 1992 May 23, Potomac, MD

Children:

3.6040 i.   Sarah Louise Marsteller
3.6041 ii.   Matthew Vance Marsteller

3.5030 Ann Cussen 6 Marsteller *(Margaret5 Louise4 Ethelburt3 Martha 2 Israel1)*
        b. 1964, DC

        m. Chris Jodlowski

3.4018 Henry Breckinridge 6 Vance *(Margaret5 Louise4 Ethelburt3 Martha 2 Israel1)*
        b. 1924 Feb 11, Lexington, KY
        d. 1966 Apr
        bur: unk

        m. Martha Elizabeth Alphin, 1948 Sep 25, Lexington, VA

Children:

3.5031 i. + Mary Gibney Vance
3.5032 ii. + Edith Webster Vance
3.5033 iii. + Henry Breckinridge Vance, Jr.
3.5034 iv. + Louise Dudley Vance
3.5035 v. + Martha Elizabeth Alphin Vance

3.5031 Mary Gibney 7 Vance *(Henry6 Margaret5 Louise4 Ethelburt3 Martha2 Israel1)*
   b. 1949

   m. Donald Roger Groth, 1978

Children:

3.6042 i. Edward Keon Vance Groth

3.5032 Edith Webster 7 Vance *(Henry6 Margaret5 Louise4 Ethelburt3 Martha2 Israel1)*
   b. 1951

   m. Terrel Adcock, 1978
   b. 1940, VA

   Son of Herbert and Faye Adcock.

Children:

3.6043 i. Scott Breckinridge Adcock
3.6044 ii. Anne Kelly Adcock   (1980)
3.6045 iii. Ryan Herbert Adcock   (1981-1988)

3.5033 Henry Breckinridge 7 Vance, Jr. *(Henry6 Margaret5 Louise4 Ethelburt3 Martha2 Israel1)*
   b. 1952

   m. Linda Kay Pederson, 1979 Nov 18

Children:

3.6046 i.   Henry Breckinridge Vance III
3.6047 ii.   Angela Marie Vance
3.6048 iii.   Nichole Elise Vance
3.6049 iv.   John Thomas Vance
3.6050 v.   Katie Vance
3.6051 vi.   Brian Vance

3.5034 Louise Dudley 7 Vance *(Henry6 Margaret5 Louise4 Ethelburt3 Martha2 Israel1)*
      b. 1954

      m. Raymond Joseph Mokszanowski, Jr., 1980 Dec 31
      b. 1953, TX

      Son of Raymond Mokszanowski, Sr. and Eva P. (Harris) Mokszanowski.

Children:

3.6052 i.   Sarah Breckinridge Mokszanowski
3.6053 ii.   Lisa Katheryn Mokszanowski

3.5035 Martha Elizabeth Alphin 7 Vance *(Henry6 Margaret5 Louise4 Ethelburt3 Martha2 Israel1)*
      b. 1955

      m. Donald Lee Robey, 1978 Aug 03
      b. 1956

Children:

3.6054 i.   Philip Breckinridge Robey
3.6055 ii.   Courtney Elizabeth Louise Robey

3.3013 John Preston 5 Breckinridge *(Louise4 Ethelburt3 Martha2 Israel1)*
      b. 1890 Oct 29, Washington, DC
      d. 1960 Jan 31, Ellicott City, MD[cxxvi]
      bur: Mt. Olivet Cemetery, Baltimore, MD (Section-A Lot-76)

      m. Varina Herbert Hanna
      b. 1887 Oct 07, MD
      d. 1978 Jul 26, Ellicott City, MD
      bur: Mt. Olivet Cemetery, Baltimore, MD (Section-A Lot-76)

3.1002 Louise "Susan" 3 Dudley *(Martha2 Israel1)*
        b. 1825 Sep 05, Lexington, KY
        d. 1901 May 24, Saratoga Springs, NY[cxxvii]
        bur: Rosse Chapel, Kenyon College, Gambier, OH (Section-1 Grave-26)

Poet; author of "Between Me and Thee"(Cleveland, Burrows Bros., 1888).[cxxviii]

        m1 John Alfred Dumont Burrows, 1843 June 08, "Elmwood", KY[cxxix]
        b. 1811 Jul 09, Elizabeth, NJ
        d. 1850 Aug 28, Cincinnati, OH[cxxx]
        bur: Spring Grove Cemetery, Cincinnati, OH (Section-106 Lot-2)

        Son of Stephen Burrows and Sarah (Meeker) Burrows. Prominent
merchant of Cincinnati.[cxxxi]

        m2 John Wesley Cracraft, 1858 Dec 01, Cincinnati, OH[cxxxii]
        b. ca. 1826, Trumbull Co., OH
        d. 1899 Oct 03, Saratoga Springs, NY[cxxxiii]
        bur: Rosse Chapel, Kenyon College, Gambier, OH (Section-1 Grave-25)

1846 graduate, Kenyon Seminary, Gambier, Ohio. Minister of the Protestant
Episcopal faith. Organized Church of the Ascension, Chicago, Illinois; Rector,
Church of the Epiphany, Philadelphia, Pennsylvania; served also at Peoria,
Illinois; Mansfield, Ohio; Hudson, Ohio; Keokuk, Iowa. Author of several
theological works, including *"The Old Paths: the Essential and the Important
Truths of the Gospel"* (Cincinnati, R. Clarke & Co., 1870);*"The Great Principles of
the Gospel"* (Philadelphia : Henry B. Ashmead, book and job printer).

Children(m1):

3.2003 i.   + Frederick Stephen Burrows
3.2004 ii.   + Margaret Ludlow Burrows
3.2005 iii.   Ambrose Dudley Burrows   (1848-1849)
3.2006 iv.   + John Alfred Dumont Burrows Jr.

Children(m2): @-adopted

3.2007 v.   Matthew Griswold Cracraft   (1859-1863)[cxxxiv]
3.2008 vi.   + Louise Dudley Cracraft
3.2009 vii. @   Amy Townsend

3.2003 Frederick Stephen 4 Burrows *(Louise4 Martha2 Israel1)*
> b. 1844 Feb --, Hamilton Co., OH
> d. 1924 Jun 15, Berkeley, CA
> bur: Erie Cemetery, Erie, PA (Section-1 Lot-12)

"At the opening of the Civil War, Major Burrows joined the 96th Ohio Volunteer Infantry and for three years campaigned in Mississippi and Louisiana. While serving in the war he was wounded twice and had many thrilling adventures."[cxxxv]

> m. Eva Josephine Wadsworth, 1874 February 07, Erie, PA
> b. 1853 Jan 30, NY
> d. 1928 Aug 13, Berkeley, CA
> bur: Erie Cemetery, Erie, PA (Section-1 Lot-12)

Children:

3.3014	i.		Robert Brown Burrows	(1874-1875)
3.3015	ii.	+	John Wadsworth Burrows	
3.3016	iii.	+	Ethelburt Dudley Burrows	

3.3015 John Wadsworth 5 Burrows *(Frederick4 Louise3 Martha2 Israel1)*
> b. 1876 Oct 25, Erie, PA
> d. 1959 Aug 09, Berkeley, CA[cxxxvi]
> bur: Golden Gate Cemetery, San Bruno, CA (Section-W site-537)

Listed in the 1900 United States census as residing in Sewickley, PA; by 1910 was living in San Francisco, CA. He served as 2nd Lt., U.S. Army during WWI. He was a Public Accountant in San Francisco.

> m1 Mabel Virginia Garrigues, 1901 Oct 17, Salem, OR (div)
> b. 1871, Salem, OR
> d. 1946 Apr 02, Berkeley, CA
> bur: Chapel of the Chimes, Oakland, CA

> m2 Katherine Owen, 1922 Feb , New York City, NY
> b. 1883 Jul 09, CA
> d. 1956 Nov 05, San Francisco, CA[cxxxvii]
> bur: Golden Gate Cemetery, San Bruno, CA (Section-W site-537)

Children(m1):

3.4019 i. + Virginia Frances Burrows

3.4019 Virginia Frances 6 Burrows *(John5 Frederick4 Louise3 Martha2 Israel1)*
   b. 1903 Mar 04, Sewickley, PA
   d. 1991 Dec 06, CA
   bur: c

   m. Kennan Clark Herrick, 1927 Apr 18, Berkeley, CA
   b. 1895 Mar 26, Riviera, CA
   d. 1985 Nov 03, Contra Costa Co., CA
   bur: Golden Gate Cemetery, San Bruno, CA (Plot-CA Grave-1768)

   Son of Alfred C. Herrick and Henrietta (Chamberlain) Herrick. Left home at about age 15 for San Francisco, California, where he was employed as a machinist's assistant. He was a diver in the U.S. Navy, ca.1917. Worked also as a machinist in Alaska and in the San Francisco bay area of California until retirement. [cxxxviii]

Children:

3.5036 i.   +   Kennan Clark Herrick, Jr.
3.5037 ii. +   David Wells Herrick
3.5038 iii. +   Joanna Herrick

3.5036 Kennan Clark 7 Herrick, Jr. *(Virginia6 John5 Frederick4 Louise3 Martha2 Israel1)*
   b. 1928, CA

Raised in Berkeley, CA; USNR 1945-46; BSEE U.C. Berkeley, 1950; variously employed as an engineer; self-employed as a sculptural artist." [cxxxix]

   m. Doris Dell Landolt, 1955 Jan 29, Alameda Co., CA
   b. 1930 Dec 12, Beaumont, TX
   d. 2011 Feb 09, Oakland, CA
   bur: c/ashes scattered

Children:

3.6056 i.   +   Colin Clyde Herrick
3.6057 ii. +   Evan Clark Herrick

3.6056 Colin Clyde 8 Herrick *(Kennan7 Virginia6 John5 Frederick4 Louise3 Martha2 Israel1)*
   b. 1955, DC

   m. Constance Lucille Johnson, 2003 Sep 27 (div)

3.6057 Evan Clark 8 Herrick *(Kennan7 Virginia6 John5 Frederick4 Louise3 Martha2 Israel1)*
b. 1959, CT

m1 Gabriele Sylvia Schafhirt, 1990 Sep 22 (div.)
b. 1951

m2 Evthalia Elizabeth Staikos
b. 1963, Germany

Children(m2):

3.7024 i.   Zoe Evangela Staikos Herrick   b. 2003, Germany

3.5037 David Wells 7 Herrick *(Virginia6 John5 Frederick4 Louise3 Martha2 Israel1)*
b. 1930 Jul 07, Alameda Co., CA
d. 2007 Apr 19, Pleasanton, CA[cxl]
bur: c

m. Elvira Alicia Bermudez, 1967 Feb 04, Alameda City, CA
b. 1930, Puerto Rico

Children:

3.6058 i.   Karin Elyse Herrick   b. 1969, CA
3.6059 ii.   David Agostino Herrick   b. 1972, CA

3.5038 Joanna 7 Herrick *(Virginia6 John5 Frederick4 Louise3 Martha2 Israel1)*
b. 1931 Sep 25, CA
d. 2007 May 20, San Rafael, CA
bur: c

m. William Henry Bycraft, 1950 Dec 24, Contra Costa Co., CA
b. 1927, CA

Son of William Morey Bycraft and Angenette Aralize (Moncrief) Bycraft.

Children:

3.6060 i.   + Julia Bycraft
3.6061 ii.   + Allison Bycraft
3.6062 iii. + William Morey Bycraft

3.6060 Julia 8 Bycraft *(Joanna7 Virginia6 John5 Frederick4 Louise3 Martha2 Israel1)*
　　　　b. 1954, CO

　　　　m. Timothy H. Cookenboo, 1986 Aug 25
　　　　b. 1958

　　　　Son of Clifton Lockett Cookenboo and Edythe (Vogen) Cookenboo.

Children:

3.7025 i.　John Jacob Cookenboo　　　　　　　b. 1989, CA
3.7026 ii.　Zoe Virginia Cookenboo　　　　　　b. 1992, CA

3.6061 Allison Bycraft
　　　　b. 1956, SC

3.6062 William Morey "Jet" 8 Bycraft *(Joanna7 Virginia6 John5 Frederick4 Louise3 Martha2 Israel1)*
　　　　b. 1958, Japan

　　　　m. Che E. Presant
　　　　b. 1956

3.3016 Ethelburt Dudley 5 Burrows *(Frederick4 Louise3 Martha2 Israel1)*
　　　　b. 1880 Aug 14, Erie, PA
　　　　d. 1931 Jul 15, San Francisco, CA[cxli]
　　　　bur: Erie Cemetery, Erie, PA (Section-1 Lot-12)

He was a "widely known newspaper man…Burrows had been drama editor of several newspapers in New York, San Francisco and the Orient."[cxlii]

　　　　m. Anne Graff Carr
　　　　b. ca 1870, Pittsburgh, PA
　　　　d. 1948 Sep 06, San Francisco, CA
　　　　bur: Erie Cemetery, Erie, PA (Section-1 Lot-12)

3.2004 Margaret Ludlow "Kate" 4 Burrows *(Louise4 Martha2 Israel1)*
　　　　b. 1845 Jun 02, Hamilton Co., OH
　　　　d. 1871 May 10, Galesburg, IL
　　　　bur: Linwood Cemetery, Galesburg, IL (Block-21 Lot-10)

　　　　m. John James Tunnicliff, 1866 Jul 03, Gambier, OH[cxliii]
　　　　b. 1841Mar 17, Penn Yan, NY
　　　　d. 1906 May 04, Galesburg, IL
　　　　bur: Linwood Cemetery, Galesburg, IL (Block-21 Lot-10)

Son of Nelson and Mary (Smith) Tunnicliff. Educated at Hamilton College, Clinton, NY, graduating in 1863. Member of the Chi Psi Fraternity. Attended Albany Law School, Albany, NY, and was admitted to the New York Bar in 1864. Removing to Illinois, he settled in Galesburg, where he entered into law partnership with Thomas Frost, one of the leading lawyers of the State of Illinois. The firm was known as Frost & Tunnicliff and remained a business until 1871 when Thomas Frost moved to Chicago. In 1872, Mr. Tunnicliff became the State's Attorney representing Knox County, a role he served for twenty years.

The Tunnicliff home was located at 663 W. North Street, Galesburg, IL.[cxliv]

Children:

| 3.3017 | i. | Louise Dudley Tunnicliff | (1868) |
| 3.3018 | ii. | Frederick Burrows Tunnicliff | (1871-1907) |

3.2006 John Alfred Dumont 4 Burrows, Jr. *(Louise3 Martha2 Israel1)*

b. 1850 Jun 07, Cincinnati, OH
d. 1920 Nov 20, Huntington, WV
bur: Spring Hill Cemetery, Charleston, WV (Section-47 Lot-6)

m. Julia Phillips Miller, 1873 Jan 21, Knoxville, IL
b. 1848 Aug 27, Peoria, IL
d. 1918 Jun 03, Charleston, WV
bur: Spring Hill Cemetery, Charleston, WV (Section-47 Lot-6)

Children:

| 3.3019 | i. | + | Frances Johnston Burrows |
| 3.3020 | ii. | + | Katherine Burrows |

3.3019 Frances Johnston "Fannie" 5 Burrows *(John4 Louise3 Martha2 Israel1)*

b. 1874 Nov 21, Little Rock, AR
d. 1960, Palm Beach, FL
bur: unk

m. P. Arthur Young, 1899 Nov 29, Charleston, WV
b 1873 May 12, Massillon, OH
d. 1955, St. Petersburg, FL
bur: unk

Son of Mortimer C. Young and Eliza Ella (Fishel) Young.

3.3020 Katherine 5 Burrows *(John4 Louise3 Martha 2 Israel1)*
  b. 1877 Dec 17, Eldorado, KS
  d. 1960 Oct 11, Wilmington, DE
  bur: Spring Hill Cemetery, Charleston, WV (Section-47 Lot-6)

  m. Ellis Thayer Crawford, 1898 Jul 20, Charleston, WV
  b. 1872 Jul 05, Charleston, WV
  d. 1937 Mar 21, Charleston, WV
  bur: Spring Hill Cemetery, Charleston, WV (Section-47 Lot-6)

Son of David Willett Crawford and Anne Ruffner Putney (Thayer). Senior member of Crawford and Ashby, a Charleston, West Virginia, real estate firm that dealt in coal and timber lands.

Children:

3.4020 i.   +   Katherine Virginia Crawford
3.4021 ii. +   William Phillips Crawford
3.4022 iii. +   Ellis Thayer Crawford, Jr.
3.4023 iv. +   Helen Elizabeth Crawford

3.4020 Katherine Virginia 6 Crawford *(Katherine5 John4 Louise3 Martha 2 Israel1)*
  b. 1899 Apr 22, Charleston, WV
  d. 1954 Apr 23, Charleston, WV[cxlv]
  bur: Mt. Moriah Cemetery, Whitehall, VA

  m. Robert Thomas Harris, 1925, Charleston, WV
  b. 1894 Nov 03, Free Union, VA
  d. 1972 May 03, Charleston, WV
  bur: Mt. Moriah Cemetery, Whitehall, VA

Son of Robert Martin Harris and Margaret Frances (Rodes) Harris.

Children:

3.5039 i   +   Robert Crawford Harris

3.5039 Robert Crawford 7 Harris *(Katherine6 Katherine5 John4 Louise3 Martha 2 Israel1)*
  b. 1930, WV

  m. Henrietta Holcomb, 1955 Mar 25, South Charleston, WV
  b. 1936, WV

Children:

3.6063 i.   +   Melanie Gail Harris
3.6064 ii. +   Robert Crawford Harris, Jr.
3.6065 iii. +   Thomas Edward Harris

3.6063 Melanie Gail Harris *(Robert7 Katherine6 Katherine5 John4 Louise3 Martha2 Israel1)*
        b. 1956, NY

        m. Anthony S. Squillante, 1981 Aug 13, Katonah, NY
        b. 1946 Dec 26, Bronx, NY
        d. 1990 May 26, White Plains, NY
        bur: Mt. Calvary Cemetery, White Plains, NY

3.6064 Robert Crawford Harris, Jr. *(Robert7 Katherine6 Katherine5 John4 Louise3 Martha2 Israel1)*
        b. 1957, OH

Graduate of State University of New York, Cortland.

        m. Nancy Jane Bradley, 1984, Pearl River, NY
        b. 1958, NY

Graduate of State University of New York, Cortland.

Children:

3.7027 i.   Melissa Susan Harris
3.7028 ii. Michael James Harris
3.7029 iii. Matthew Alexander Harris

3.6065 Thomas Edward Harris *(Robert7 Katherine6 Katherine5 John4 Louise3 Martha2 Israel1)*
        b. 1964, OH

        m. Cynthia Marie Bonds, 1987 May 17, Mt. Kisco, NY (div.)
        b. 1964, Mexico

Children:

3.7030 i.   Tricia Michelle Harris
3.7031 ii. Ashley Elizabeth Harris

3.4021 William Phillips 6 Crawford *(Katherine5 John4 Louise3 Martha2 Israel1)*
  b. 1900 Nov 23, Charleston, WV
  d. 1977 Mar 12, Scottsdale, AZ[cxlvi]
  bur: Spring Hill Cemetery (Section-47 Lot-6)

Graduate of the Colorado School of Mines, 1922; Superintendant of the Eagle Mine at White Pine, Colorado.[cxlvii] "Superintendant of the Phelps Dodge Corporation open-pit mine, Bisbee, AZ."[cxlviii]

  m. Maytee Pearl Eden, 1920 May 29, Denver, CO
  b. 1902 Sep 12, Morrison, CO
  d. 1993 Mar 23, Bisbee, AZ
  bur: Peru Cemetery, Peru, IA

Children:

3.5040 i.   +   Ellis Eden Crawford
3.5041 ii.   +   Patricia Lee Crawford

3.5040 Ellis Eden "Bill" 7 Crawford *(William6 Katherine5 John4 Louise3 Martha2 Israel1)*
  b. 1923 Oct 33, Montrose, CO
  d. 2006 Sep 03, AZ
  bur: unk

  m. Betty Lucille Richmond
  b. 1921 Jun 06, CO
  d. 2006 Feb 18, Bisbee, AZ
  bur: unk

Children:

3.6066 i.   Linda Crawford
3.6067 ii.   Phillip Steven Crawford
3.6068 iii.   Michael E. Crawford

3.5041 Patricia Lee 7 Crawford *(William6 Katherine5 John4 Louise3 Martha2 Israel1)*
  b. 1931 May 07, Bisbee, AZ
  d. 2006 Apr 28, Scottsdale, AZ
  bur: Peru Cemetery, Peru, IA

  m. Thomas Daniel Fridena, Jr.
  b. 1929, AZ

Son of Thomas D. Fridena, Sr. and Marie J.

Children:

3.6069 i.   +   Eden Marie Fridena

3.6069 Eden Marie 8 Fridena *(Patricia7 William6 Katherine5 John4 Louise3 Martha2 Israel1)*
         b. 1957, AZ

Graduated Scottsdale High School, 1975; Bachelor's degree, University of Arizona, 1979; earned her Ph.D from Iowa State University.

         m. Mark Robert Pearson, 1978 May 20, Phoenix, AZ
         b. 1957 Sep 08, Lafayette, IN
         d. 2012 Jun 03, East Peru, IA
         bur: Peru Cemetery, Peru, IA

         Son of Robert and June Pearson. Graduate of Naperville Central High School, Naperville, IL, 1975; graduated University of Arizona, Tucson, 1979, majoring in journalism. Member of the Phi Gamma Delta Fraternity. Entered the United States Naval Reserves in 1986 and attained the rank of Lieutenant Commander. Served as Assistant Secretary of Agriculture for the State of Iowa.

Children:

3.7032 i.	Michael Mark Pearson	b. 1984, IA
3.7033 ii.	Katherine Marie Pearson	b. 1986, IA
3.7034 iii.	Elizabeth Eden Pearson	b. 1990, IA
3.7035 iv.	Mary Ellice Pearson	b. 1997, IA

3.4022 Ellis Thayer 6 Crawford, Jr. *(Katherine5 John4 Louise3 Martha2 Israel1)*
         b. 1906 Nov 16, Charleston, WV
         d. 1942 Jun 01, Providence, RI
         bur: Spring Hill Cemetery, Charleston, WV (Section-47 Lot-6)

Graduate of the University of Cincinnati and member of the Triangle and Sigma Sigma fraternities. Metallurgist, Carbide and Carbon Chemicals Corporation.

         m. Ora Alice Easterday, 1933 Dec 23, Charleston, WV[cxlix]
         b. 1906 Jul 16, Fergus Falls, MN
         d. 1979 May 25, Chicago, IL
         bur: Spring Hill Cemetery, Charleston, WV (Section-47 Lot-6)

Graduate of Ohio State University, Columbus. "Nursing career: WV public health/school nurse; industrial nurse, Union Carbide plants, South Charleston, WV; Associate Professor of Nursing, University of Charleston."[cl]

Children:

3.5042 i.   + Bruce Donald Crawford
3.5043 ii. + Carol Louise Crawford

3.5042 Bruce Donald 7 Crawford *(Ellis6 Katherine5 John4 Louise3 Martha2 Israel1)*
     b. 1936, WV

Graduate of West Virginia University, 1960.

     m. Miriam Alice Hall, 1960 Jun 26, New Martinsville, WV[cli]
     b. 1941, WV

Graduate of West Virginia University, 1972.

Children:

3.6070 i.   + Sybil Louise Crawford
3.6071 ii.   Eric Thayer Crawford   (1963-1988)

3.6070 Sybil Louise Crawford
     b. 1962, PA

Ph.D in Statistics from Carnegie-Mellon University, Pittsburgh, PA. Epidemiologist and Associate Professor, University of Massachusetts Medical School, Worcester.

     m. Peter Mooney, 2010 Jan 11, Hudson, MA

Children: @-adopted

3.7036 i. @ Benjamin A. Crawford   b. 2005, Ethiopia

3.5043 Carol Louise 7 Crawford *(Ellis6 Katherine5 John4 Louise3 Martha2 Israel1)*
     b. 1939, WV

     m. Ronald Keith Gibbs, 1959 Sep 05, Charleston, WV
     b. 1937, WV

Children:

3.6072 i.   Jeffrey Gibbs
3.6073 ii.   Steven Gibbs
3.6074 iii.   Daniel Gibbs

3.4023 Helen Elizabeth 6 Crawford *(Katherine5 John4 Louise3 Martha 2 Israel1)*
>   b. 1908 Dec 08, Charleston, WV
>   d. 1983 Nov 11, Delray Beach, FL
>   bur: Spring Hill Cemetery, Charleston, WV (Section-47 Lot-6)
>
>   m. David Morris Hurt, 1930 May 20, Charleston, WV[clii]
>   b. 1904 Mar 28, Illiopolis, IL
>   d. 1971 Jan --, Severna Park, MD
>   bur: Spring Hill Cemetery, Charleston, WV (Section-47 Lot-6)
>
>   Son of Joseph Hurt. An associate of the DuPont Ammonia Corp.

Children:

3.5044 i.   + Anna Katherine Hurt
3.5045 ii.   + David Morris Crawford Hurt

3.5044 Anna Katherine 7 Hurt *(Helen6 Katherine5 John4 Louise3 Martha 2 Israel1)*
>   b. 1933, WV
>
>   m1 Oscar Donald Steppler, 1953 Jan 03, Elkton, MD (div., 1956)
>   m2 Edwin John Nilsson, 1961 Jun 13, Ft. Lauderdale, FL (div., 1974)
>   m3 Lloyd Charles Johnson, 1981 Jan 30, Delray Beach, FL

Children(m2):

3.6075 i.   Katherine Phillips Nilsson

3.6075 Katherine Phillips Nilsson
>   b. 1964 Aug 16, Wilmington, DE
>   d. 1994 Aug 08
>   bur: unk
>
>   m. Stephen Hiday Teetor, 1981 May 02, Ft. Lauderdale, FL
>   b. 1953
>
>   Son of Benjamin Jessup Teetor and Margie (Hiday) Teetor.

Children:

3.7037 i.	Sarah Johnson Teetor	b. 1982, NC
3.7038 ii.	Benjamin Johnson Teetor	b. 1984, NC

3.5045 David Morris Crawford Hurt
        b. 1936, OH

        m. Joan Jackson, 1964 Aug 09, Newark, DE

Children:

| 3.6076 | i. | David William Hurt | b. 1966, FL |
| 3.6077 | ii. | Valerie Elaine Hurt | b. 1969, MD |

3.2008 Louise Dudley 4 Cracraft *(Louise4 Martha 2 Israel1)*
        b. 1876 Sep 01, Peoria, IL
        d. 1938 Apr 29, Columbus, OH
        bur: Rosse Chapel, Kenyon College, Gambier, OH (Section-1 Plot-24A)

        m. George P. Updegraff, 1892 Sep 28, Wayne Co., OH

3.1003 Charlotte A. 3 Dudley *(Martha 2 Israel1)*
        b. 1829 May --, KY
        d. 1881 Oct 12, St. Louis, St, MO
        bur: Spring Grove Cemetery, Cincinnati, OH (Section-35 Lot-178)

        m. Lafayette Armstrong, 1845 Oct 15, Cincinnati, OH[cliii]
        b. 1824 Jun 19, Lexington, KY
        d. 1909 Mar 11, Lexington, KY
        bur: Lexington Cemetery, Lexington, KY (Section-F Lot-81)

        Son of Andrew Armstrong and Jane (Cavins) Armstrong.

3.1004 Ellen Catherine 3 Dudley *(Martha 2 Israel1)*
        b. 1831 Jan 14, Cincinnati, OH
        d. 1909 Aug 22, Indianapolis, IN[cliv]
        bur: Spring Grove Cemetery, Cincinnati, OH (Section-35 Lot-178)

        m1 Littleton E. Bennett
        b. ca. 1822, Augusta, KY
        d. 1852 Oct 01, Newport, KY[clv]
        bur: unk

        Son of John Bennett, Kentucky State Senator. Served as 1st Lt., Co. E,
2nd Kentucky Infantry during the Mexican War. Physician.

m2 Francis W. Major, 1854 Mar 08, Gambier, OH[clvi]
    b. 1814 Apr 02, Frankfort, KY
    d. 1886 Mar 24, Frankfort, KY
    bur: Spring Grove Cemetery, Cincinnati, OH (Section-35 Lot-178)

Son of George and Mary (Bowman) Major. Physician.

Children(m1):

3.2010 i.   Ambrose Dudley Bennett   (1850-1851) [clvii]

Children(m2):

3.2011 ii.   William Rufus Major   (1854-1882)
3.2012 iii. + Charlotte Major

3.2012 Charlotte 4 Major *(Ellen 3 Martha 2 Israel 1)*
    b. 1856 Mar 02, Covington, KY
    d. 1934 Mar 19, San Bernardino, CA
    bur: Spring Grove Cemetery, Cincinnati, OH (Section-35 Lot-178)

    m. Robert C. Auld, 1882 Jul 22
    b. 1846 Jul 07, Belfast, Ireland
    d. 1900 Jul 27, Chattanooga, TN
    bur: National Cemetery of Chattanooga, TN (Section-S Grave-13334)

    Son of Samuel Auld and Anna (Connelly) Auld.
During the Civil War, he enlisted in Company Battery L, Illinois 2nd LA Battery L
Light Artillery Battery on 23 Feb 1864. Mustered out of service 9 Aug 1865 at
Chicago, IL.

Children:

3.3021 i.   Robert Major Auld   (1884-1885)
3.3022 ii.   John Auld   (1886-1891)
3.3023 iii. + Ellen Auld
3.3024 iv. + Mildred Auld
3.3025 v. + Frank Stewart Auld

3.3023 Ellen "Nell" 5 Auld *(Charlotte4 Ellen3 Martha2 Israel1)*
    b. 1888 Jan 01, IL
    d. 1969 May 29, San Pedro, CA
    bur: Spring Grove Cemetery, Cincinnati, OH (Section-35 Lot-178)

m. Verne Rodell Campbell, 1908
b. 1878 Oct 23, MI
d. 1953 Jan 16, Long Beach, CA
bur: Spring Grove Cemetery, Cincinnati, OH (Section-35 Lot-178)

Son of William Campbell and Helen (Austin) Campbell.

Children:

3.4024 i.　　+　Frances Elaine Campbell
3.4025 ii.　　+　MaryVerne Campbell

3.4024 Frances Elaine 6 Campbell *(Ellen5 Charlotte4 Ellen3 Martha2 Israel1)*
b. 1909 Mar 29, Bellevue, KY
d. 1994 May 13, Porterville, CA
bur: c

m. Roman Stanley Wasielewski, 1943 Apr 03
b. 1904 Feb 02, Anoka, MN
d. 1992 May 03, Phoenix, AZ
bur: National Memorial Cemetery of Arizona (Section-38A Site 94)

Son of Antoni and Anna (Blosky) Wasielewski. Served in the United States Coast Guard, 1942-43, exiting service with a rank of S2 (E-2)."[clviii]

Children:

3.5046 i.　　+　Ron Campbell
3.5047 ii.　　+　Celine Suzanne Bruneau

Children(m1):

3.5048 iii.　　+　Antoni Frank. Wasielewski
3.5049 iv.　　+　Nikolas Jon Wasielewski
3.5050 v.　　+　Lisa Anne Wasielewski

3.5046 Ron 7 Campbell *(Frances6 Ellen5 Charlotte4 Ellen3 Martha2 Israel1)*
b. 1937, IN

Served in the U.S. Army, 1954-1957.

3.5047 Celine Suzanne 7 Bruneau *(Frances6 Ellen5 Charlotte4 Ellen3 Martha2 Israel1)*
b. 1940, AZ

Served in the U.S. Army, 1972-80, 1984-85; U.S. Coast Guard, 1981-1983.

m. Theodore Cecil Proudfit, 1960 Apr 01, Menlo Park, CA

Son of Charles Cecil Proudfit and Dorothea (Bullis) Proudfit.
Served in the U.S. Army Reserve, 1960-63.

Children:

3.6078	i.	Tamera Celine Proudfit	b. 1961, CA
3.6079	ii.	Tanya Michelle Proudfit	b. 1962, CA
3.6080	iii.	Bradford Theodore Proudfit	b. 1965, CA
3.6081	iv.	+ Erich Curtis Proudfit	

3.6081 Erich Curtis 8 Proudfit *(Celine7 Frances6 Ellen5 Charlotte4 Ellen3 Martha2 Israel1)*
b. 1966, CA

m. Leslie Wolper
b. 1964

Children:

| 3.7039 | i. | Amy Elizabeth Proudfit | b. 2005, CA |

3.5048 Antoni Frank 7 Wasielweski *(Frances6 Ellen5 Charlotte4 Ellen3 Martha2 Israel1)*
b. 1944 Apr 12, Phoenix, AZ
d. 2010 Aug 03, Shelbyville, KY
bur: National Memorial Cemetery of Arizona

Served in the USAF between 1963-1971; achieved the rank of Technical
Sergeant (E-6). [clix]

m1 Jane Dunshee, 1963 Jul 12
b. 1945 Dec 28, Phoenix, AZ
d. 1977 Dec 04, Phoenix, AZ
bur: St. Francis Cemetery, Phoenix, AZ

m2 Waltraud Rachel Ziegler
b. 1952 Apr 02, Berlin, Germany
d. 2002 Oct 23, Mesa, AZ
bur: National Memorial Cemetery of Arizona

Children(m1):

3.6082 i.   +   Shawn Wasielewski
3.6083 ii. +   Shannon Wasielewski
3.6084 iii. +   Kyle Wasielewski

Children(m2):

3.6085 iv. +   Mara Wasielewski
3.6086 v.   +   Ryan Wasielewski
3.6087 vi. +   Ashley Wasielewski

3.6082 Shawn 8 Wasielewski *(Antoni7 Frances6 Ellen5 Charlotte4 Ellen3 Martha2 Israel1)*
        b. 1964, MS

        m. Catherine Bache
        b. 1955

Children:

3.7040 i.   Brittany Wasielewski   b. 1989, AZ
3.7041 ii.   Kristopher Wasielewski   b. 1990, AZ
3.7042 iii.   Randi Wasielewski   b. 1991, AZ

3.6083 Shannon 8 Wasielewski *(Antoni7 Frances6 Ellen5 Charlotte4 Ellen3 Martha2 Israel1)*
        b. 1966, TX

        m. Michelle Wilson, 2004 Jun 04, Tucson, AZ
        b. 1968, AZ

Children:

3.7043 i.   Jennifer Wasielewski   b. 2004, AZ
3.7044 ii.   Jacob Wasielewski   b. 2005, AZ
3.7045 iii.   George Wasielewski   b. 2008, AZ

3.6084 Kyle 8 Wasielewski *(Antoni7 Frances6 Ellen5 Charlotte4 Ellen3 Martha2 Israel1)*
        b. 1970, Germany

        m. Dolly Alex, 2004 Aug 16, Roche Harbor, WA
        b. 1969, India

3.6085 Mara 8 Wasielewski *(Antoni7 Frances6 Ellen5 Charlotte4 Ellen3 Martha2 Israel1)*
>   b. 1980, AZ

>   m. Garrett Lavoie

Children:

3.7046 i.   Theron Levoie   b. 2007, KY

3.6086 Ryan 8 Wasielewski *(Antoni7 Frances6 Ellen5 Charlotte4 Ellen3 Martha2 Israel1)*
>   b.1981, AZ

3.6087 Ashley 8 Wasielewski *(Antoni7 Frances6 Ellen5 Charlotte4 Ellen3 Martha2 Israel1)*
>   b. 1983, CA

3.5049 Nikolas Jon "Nik" 7 Wasielewski *(Frances6 Ellen5 Charlotte4 Ellen3 Martha2 Israel1)*
>   b. 1945

>   m. Patricia Kapaldo

Children:

3.6088 i.   Buffy Wasielewski   b. 1970
3.6089 ii.   Christopher Wasielewski   b. 1973

3.5050 Lisa Anne 7 Wasielewski *(Frances6 Ellen5 Charlotte4 Ellen3 Martha2 Israel1)*
>   b. 1948, AZ

>   m. Michael Frederick Rost, 1967 Jun 04, Phoenix, AZ
>   b. 1939, MI

>   Son of Scherline "Steve" Frederick Rost and Florence Irene (Powers).
> Served in the U.S. Marines Reserve, 1961-66, 9th Engineers, CPL.

Children:

3.6090 i.   Tammera Anne Rost   b. 1969, AZ
3.6091 ii.   + Audra Marie Rost
3.6092 iii.   Leland Frederick Rost   b.1977, CA
3.6093 iv.   + Corinna Lee Rost

3.6091 Audra Marie 8 Rost *(Lisa7 Frances6 Ellen5 Charlotte4 Ellen3 Martha2 Israel1)*
>   b. 1971, CA

m. Brian Carroll Kirby, 1990 Nov 24, Springville, CA
b. 1968, CA

Son of Frank Carroll Kirby and Katherine Ann (Gannaway) Kirby.

Children:

3.7047 i.　　Marnae Lynn Kirby　　　　　b. 1992, CA
3.7048 ii.　　Alexandra Nicole Kirby　　　b. 1995, CA

3.6093 Corinna Lee 8 Rost *(Lisa7 Frances6 Ellen5 Charlotte4 Ellen3 Martha2 Israel1)*
　　　　b. 1978, CA

　　　　m. Erik Hendrix, 2000 Jun 14, Merksem, Antwerpen, Belgium
　　　　b. 1973, Belgium

　　　　Son of Henri Francois Hendrix and Magdaline Josepha (Vermeyen).

Children:

3.7049 i.　　Colin Henri Hendrix　　　　　b. 2005, CA
3.7050 ii.　　Ethan Michael Hendrix　　　　b. 2005, CA

3.4025 MaryVerne 6 Campbell *(Ellen5 Charlotte4 Ellen3 Martha2 Israel1)*
　　　　b. 1911 Jun 19, IN
　　　　d. 1998 Jun 25, Tucson, AZ
　　　　bur: c

　　　　m. Granville Conner III
　　　　b. 1903
　　　　d. 1978 Oct 29, Miami, FL
　　　　bur: unk

Children:

3.5049 i.　　+　Granville Conner IV

3.5049 Granville 7 Conner IV *(MaryVerne6 Ellen5 Charlotte4 Ellen3 Martha2 Israel1)*
　　　　b. 1938, FL

　　　　m. Jane E. Turgeon, 1959 Mar 13, Los Angeles, CA
　　　　b. 1939 Aug 23
　　　　d. 2011 May 09, Newport Beach, CA
　　　　bur: unk

(=) Diane Calvitti

Children(m):

3.6094 i.   Lisa Colleen Conner   b. 1959, CA

Children(=):

3.6095 i.   + Roderick Anthony Conner

3.6095 Roderick Anthony "Michael" 8 Conner *(Granville7 Mary Verne6 Ellen5 Charlotte4 Ellen3 Martha2 Israel1)*

Children:

3.7051 i.   Brandon Lee Conner
3.7052 ii.   Michael Ashton Conner

3.3026 Mildred "Dixie" 5 Auld *(Charlotte4 Ellen3 Martha2 Israel1)*
       b. 1892 Feb 27, Chattanooga, TN
       d. 1975 Nov 28, San Bernardino, CA
       bur: Mt. View Cemetery, San Bernardino, CA

       m. Albert Russell Easterday, 1917 Apr 28, Hancock, IN
       b. 1896 May 05, Center, IN
       d. 1976 Jun 12, San Bernardino, CA
       bur: Mt. View Cemetery, San Bernardino, CA

       Son of Joseph Wise Easterday and Emma (Ross) Easterday.

Children:

3.4026 i.   Dixie Lee Easterday
3.4027 ii.   Russell Easterday

3.3027 Frank Stewart 5 Auld *(Charlotte4 Ellen3 Martha2 Israel1)*
       b. 1895 Mar 23, Chattanooga, TN
       d. 1985 Oct 31, Tulsa, OK
       bur: Rose Hill Memorial Park Cemetery, Tulsa, OK

       m1 Terressa Shields
       b. 1894 Nov 30, Pineville, MO
       d. 1972 Jan 24, Tulsa, OK
       bur: Rose Hill Memorial Park Cemetery, Tulsa, OK

m2 Ona Truett (Rowsey) Spillman, 1973, Tulsa, OK
b. 1901 Feb 03, Pike, TX
d. 1998 Apr 17, Tulsa, OK
bur: Rose Hill Memorial Park Cemetery, Tulsa, OK (Section 14 Lot-603)

Children (m1):

3.4028 i.   +   Terressa Frances Auld
3.4029 ii. +   Stuart Donald Auld

3.4028 Terressa Frances 6 Auld *(Frank5 Charlotte4 Ellen3 Martha2 Israel1)*
b. 1924 Nov --, OK
d. 1980 Aug 01, Tulsa, OK
bur: Rose Hill Memorial Park, Tulsa, OK

m1 ---- Van Horn
m2 Wayne Eugene Myers

Children(m1):

3.5050 i.   +   Janet L'eva Catherine Myers
3.5051 ii. +   Terressa Shirley Myers

3.5050 Janet L'eva Catherine 7 Myers *(Terressa6 Frank5 Charlotte4 Ellen3 Martha2 Israel1)*
b. 1949 May 10, Tulsa, OK
d. 2013 Aug 02, Wagoner, OK
bur: Rose Hill Memorial Park, Tulsa, OK

3.5051 Terressa Shirley 7 Myers *(Terressa6 Frank5 Charlotte4 Ellen3 Martha2 Israel1)*
b. 1951, OK

3.4029 Stuart Donald 6 Auld *(Frank5 Charlotte4 Ellen3 Martha2 Israel1)*
b. 1930 Sep 03, Detroit, MI
d. 1995 Dec 03, New Orleans, LA
bur: Metairie Cemetery

m1 Marilyn Lowe
m2 Evelyn Gaspard, 1969 Dec 13, New Orleans, LA
b. 1941 Feb 01, New Orleans, LA

Children(m1): @-adopted

3.5052 i. @   Phillip Stuart Auld   b. 1955
3.5053 ii.   Stuart Charles Auld   b. 1964, NM

Louise Ludlow Dudley Breckinridge with children

L-R, Ethelburt, Margaret [on lap], Mary, Lucian, Scott Dudley and Lucy [on floor]
"Photograph taken for Joseph Cabell Breckinridge [Jr.] at U.S.N.A. (1888?)
Watch photo of Joseph Cabell Breckinridge [Sr.] pasted over mantel"

Photo courtesy of Susan Kneass Laursen

George Bryan Kneass, Jr.
Photo courtesy of Susan Kneass Laursen

Anita Wood and George Bryan Kneass, Jr.
Photo courtesy of Susan Kneass Laursen

George Bryan Kneass, Sr.
Photo courtesy of Susan Kneass Laursen

Louise Ludlow Dudley Hines Kneass.
Photo courtesy of Susan Kneass Laursen

Captain John Fore Hines

Photo courtesy of Susan Kneass Laursen

McLean-Garrard Grave Markers

The obelisk in the foreground marks the grave of John McLean. Horizontal stone in the back, at right, marks the grave of Sarah Bella McLean. Between the two is the Garrard marker in the center.

Spring Grove Cemetery
Section 99 Lots 1 & 2

Sarah Bella Ludlow

4.0001   Sarah Bella ₂ Ludlow *(Israel1)*
            b. 1802, "Ludlow Station"[clx], OH
            d. 1882 Jan 13, Cincinnati, OH[clxi]
            bur: Spring Grove Cemetery, Cincinnati, OH (Section-99 Lot-2)

Named after her maternal aunt, Sarah Bella (Chambers) Dunlop, Sarah Bella Ludlow was described in her childhood as a "fair-haired, bright-eyed girl, a perfect blonde".[clxii]
As an adult she was active in many causes including charities, community and church organizations and especially in the abolition movement.
      "During the anti-slavery movement she was one of its most able exponents in this city [Cincinnati] *, and to her efforts the institution of the Cincinnati Orphan Asylum is greatly due. She was a woman whose heart never failed to respond to the call of charity."* [clxiii]
 Her first husband, Jeptha Dudley Garrard, had an established law practice in Cincinnati, and during their marriage, they became the parents of four sons. Their residence in Cincinnati was located on East Fourth Street.
Six years after the untimely death of her first husband, Sarah Bella married John McLean, and moved to Washington, DC. McLean, a prominent politician had been appointed Postmaster General of the United States by President James Monroe, followed by an appointment to the Supreme Court by President Andrew Jackson. Judge McLean opposed the practice of slavery and its expansion into the American west... views strongly supported by Sarah Bella. Prominent in Washington, DC society, Sarah Bella "always appeared as a charming and elegant woman", and she was undoubtedly a driving force behind Mr. McLean's political ambitions. She corresponded with influential people of her time, and was universally respected and admired.[clxiv]
After the death of her second husband, in 1861, Sarah Bella McLean traveled often to visit her sons in Cincinnati, New York and Minnesota.
She lived for a time in the Clifton area of Cincinnati and for sixteen years near her sons in Frontenac, Minnesota, where her home there was known as "Greystone".
At the time of her sudden and unexpected death, she was staying at Cincinnati's celebrated hotel, the Burnet House. Her funeral was held at Cincinnati's Central Christian Church, where she was one of its "best and oldest members".

m1 Jeptha Dudley Garrard, 1824 Jun 25
b. 1802 Dec 05, "Fairfield", Bourbon Co., KY
d. 1837 Jan 26, Cincinnati, OH[clxv]
bur: Spring Grove Cemetery, Cincinnati, OH (Section-99 Lot-2)

Son of Gen. James and Nancy (Lewis) Garrard. Grandson of Kentucky Governor James Garrard. Studied law at Transylvania College, Lexington, Kentucky. Established his law practice in Cincinnati, Ohio.
"Few men in our company were more valued by the friends that knew them; few could be called from us who will be more missed---and most of all, missed by the poor and needy. Even now not a few hearths are cold and comfortless, which would have been far otherwise had not death called Jeptha D. Garrard to his last account."[clxvi]

m2 John McLean, 1843 May 11, Cincinnati, OH[clxvii]
b. 1785 Mar 11, Morris Co., NJ
d. 1861 Apr 04, Washington, DC[clxviii]
bur: Spring Grove Cemetery, Cincinnati, OH (Section-99 Lot-1)

Son of Fergus and Sophia (Blockford) McLean. By 1807, he was living in Warren County, Ohio, where he founded a weekly newspaper, "The Western Star". He read law and was admitted to the bar that same year. He was elected to the Ohio Supreme Court, resigning that position in 1822 to accept President James Monroe's appointment as Commissioner of the General Land Office. In 1823, he was appointed by Monroe as the United States Postmaster General, serving between 1823-1829. In 1829, President Andrew Jackson appointed McLean to the Supreme Court. He was considered as a candidate for the Republican party nomination in the presidential election of 1856, and again in 1860, however, John C. Fremont was nominated in the former and Abraham Lincoln in the latter.
McLean was well-known for his opposition to slavery, particularly apparent in cases such as "Dred Scott v. Sandford", among others.[clxix]

Children(m1):

4.1001	i.	+	Israel Garrard	
4.1002	ii.	+	Kenner Garrard	
4.1003	iii.	+	Lewis Hector Garrard	
4.1004	iv.	+	Jeptha Dudley Garrard, Jr.	

Children(m2):

| 4.1005 | v. | | Ludlow McLean | (1846) |

4.1001 Israel 3 Garrard *(Sarah 2 Israel 1)*
      b. 1825 Oct 22, "Fairfield", Bourbon Co.KY
      d. 1901 Sep 21, Frontenac, MN[clxx]
      bur: Old Frontenac Cemetery, Frontenac, MN

Educated at Cary's College; Bethany College and Harvard University, he went into the practice of law at Cincinnati. In October of 1854, he and his brother Lewis ascended the Mississippi River from Kentucky on a hunting trip and camped on a bluff overlooking Lake Pepin. The site pleased him and, within a few years, he had acquired several hundred acres of the property. His home there was named "St. Hubert's Lodge". A town was platted, containing 320 acres, which was officially named "Frontenac" on September 13, 1859.[clxxi]
At the beginning of the Civil War, Garrard returned to Cincinnati; was commissioned Colonel in command of the 7th Ohio Volunteer Cavalry on September 18th, 1862, and went into the field with the Army of Ohio. Joining General Burnside, he took command of a brigade in Kentucky.
He served with General Sherman during his march to the sea and was commander of the cavalry of the Army of Ohio through that campaign. He also served in the campaign of Nashville under General Thomas, which resulted in the destruction of General Hood's Confederate Army.
In recognition of his distinguished duty, Israel Garrard was brevetted Brigadier General of the U.S. Volunteers on the 20th of June, 1865.
After the war, he returned to Frontenac to live for the remainder of his life.

      m. Catharine "Kate" Wood, 1856
      b. 1835
      d. 1867 Jan 12
      bur: Old Frontenac Cemetery, Frontenac, MN

Children:

4.2001 i.   + Margaret Hills Garrard
4.2002 ii. + George Wood Garrard
4.2003 iii.   K. H. Wood Garrard (1867)

4.2001 Margaret Hills 4 Garrard *(Israel 3 Sarah 2 Israel 1)*
      b. 1857
      d. 1934
      bur: Woodland Cemetery, Bellport, NY

4.2002 George Wood ₄ Garrard *(Israel₃ Sarah ₂ Israel₁)*
        b. 1863 Aug 20, Peekskill, NY
        d. 1928 Mar 25, Los Angeles, CA
        bur: Old Frontenac Cemetery, Frontenac, MN

Educated at Morgan Park Military Academy, Chicago, IL. He traveled extensively throughout Europe and the Far East, studying for a year at Tours, France. He also lived for a year at Brighton, England, and two years at Brussels, Belgium. He returned to live in Minnesota, becoming the manager and owner of the Frontenac Stone Company.
His home in Frontenac was called "Winona Cottage". [clxxii]

        m. Virginia Golden Hoffman, 1889 Oct 31, New York, NY
        b. 1864 Feb 27, NY
        d. 1951 Feb 21, Washington, DC[clxxiii]
        bur: Old Frontenac Cemetery, Frontenac, MN

Children:

4.3001 i.	+	Beulah Murray Garrard
4.3002 ii.	+	Evelyn Stuart Garrard
4.3003 iii.	+	Catharine Wood Garrard

4.3001 Beulah Murray ₅ Garrard *(George₄ Israel₃ Sarah ₂ Israel₁)*
        b. 1893 Jan 07, Albany, NY[clxxiv]
        d. 1965 Apr 27, Hampstead, London, England
        bur: c

        m. Leonard Charles Beecroft, 1918 January 17, Hartford, CT
        b. 1887 Jan 18, Luton, Bedfordshire, England
        d. 1953 Nov 24, Hampstead, London, England
        bur: c

Son of Frederic Beecroft. Prior to WWI, he met his future wife while on vacation in Switzerland, and they became engaged. Later, while serving in the British Army during the war, he obtained leave to travel to the United States in 1918 to marry his fiancée.
In civilian life, he was a chartered accountant. [clxxv]

Children:

| 4.4001 i. | + | Murray Garrard Beecroft |
| 4.4002 ii. | + | Kenner Stanley Beecroft |

4.4001 Murray Garrard 6 Beecroft *(Beulah5 George4 Israel3 Sarah 2 Israel1)*
   b. 1925
   d. 2011
   bur: ----

Educated at Westminster School, London, and Christ Church, Oxford; joined the Royal Air Force in 1942 and trained as a pilot, leaving the service in 1952." [clxxvi]

4.4002 Kenner Stanley 6 Beecroft *(Beulah5 George4 Israel3 Sarah 2 Israel1)*
   b. 1930, England

"Educated at Harrow School, London; qualified as a chartered accountant in 1952 and entered into public practice in 1956. Retired in 1990 as a senior partner in the UK firm of Deloitte. The last twenty years of his professional career were largely spent in the international management of the business. He undertook military service from 1952 to 1954, was commissioned into the Royal Fusiliers and spent the majority of this time on secondment to the King's African Rifles in central Africa.' [clxxvii]

   m1 Margaret MacDonald Drummond, 1954, Zomba, Nyasaland
   m2 Sondra Kaye Boyles Miller, 1983, London, England

Children(m1):

4.5001 i.   +   Carol Ann Beecroft   b. 1954, England
4.5002 ii. +   Belinda Jane Beecroft   b. 1956, England

4.5001 Carol Ann 7 Beecroft *(Kenner6 Beulah5 George4 Israel3 Sarah 2 Israel1)*
   b. 1954, England

   m. Stuart Andrew Bayford, 1977
   b. 1955

Children:

4.6001 i.   Daniel Andrew Bayford   b. 1982, England
4.6002 ii.   Stephanie Ann Bayford   b. 1983, England
4.6003 iii.   Caroline Amanda Bayford   b. 1985, England

4.5002 Belinda Jane 7 Beecroft *(Kenner6 Beulah5 George4 Israel3 Sarah 2 Israel1)*
   b. 1956

   m. David Smithson, 1979, London, England (div.)

Children:

4.6004	i.	Adam Kenner Smithson	b. 1981, England
4.6005	ii.	Garry Kenner Beecroft	b. 1983, England
4.6006	iii.	Oliver Marcus Beecroft	b. 1989, England

4.3002 Evelyn Stuart 5 Garrard *(George4 Israel3 Sarah 2 Israel1)*
> b. 1895 Jul 21, Frontenac, MN
> d. 1991 Feb 02, Fairfax, VA
> bur: Arlington National Cemetery, Arlington, VA (Section-8 6060-5-LH)

> m1 Lewis Haas Starnes (div. ca. 1925)
> b. 1890 Apr 02, KS
> d. 1931 Jul 26
> bur: unk

Son of Pleasant Mitchell Starnes and Marie (Lower).

> m2 Emanuel Chester Beck, 1927 Nov 11, Pensacola, FL
> b. 1897 Jan 18, York, PA
> d. 1987 Feb 24, Fairfax, VA
> bur: Arlington National Cemetery, Arlington, VA (Section-8 6060-5-LH)

Son of Augustus Beck and Maude (Gipe) Beck. "Attended the Carnegie Institute of Technology, Pittsburgh, PA; graduated from the U.S. Naval Academy, Annapolis, MD, in 1919. He served aboard cruisers and destroyers and received flight training and was a flight instructor at Pensacola, FL, in 1927. Also in that year he received letters of commendation from the governors of Arkansas and Louisiana for his participation in Mississippi River flood relief flight duty. He retired in 1930.
After studying at the London School of Economics, he worked in banking and industry, until recalled to active duty.
He was recalled for the office of the Assistant Secretary of the Navy for Air from 1948 to 1949." [clxxviii]

Children(m1):

4.4003 i.   + Lewis Israel Garrard

Children(m2):

4.4004 ii.   + Stuart Morgan Beck

4.4003 Lewis Israel 6 Garrard* *(Evelyn5 George4 Israel3 Sarah 2 Israel1)*
   b. 1920 Oct 28
   d. 1991 Jun 16, Olmsted Co., MN
   bur: Old Frontenac Cemetery, Frontenac, MN

*Born as Lewis Israel Starnes, he was adopted by his stepfather and given the surname Beck (ca. 1929).
Received his M.A. and B.A. degrees from the University of Minnesota.
Served as a member of the Frontenac Historical Society. His home, which was the converted first Post Office building of Frontenac, Minnesota, is listed on the National Register of Historic Places.
In later years (ca. 1983) he changed his name to Lewis Israel Garrard. [clxxix]

   m. Anita Evelyn Frajola

Children:

4.5003 i.   Peter Garrard Beck
4.5004 ii.   Michael Garrard Beck

4.4004 Stuart Morgan 6 Beck *(Evelyn5 George4 Israel3 Sarah 2 Israel1)*
   b. 1928, FL

   m. Lola Fares Sarofim, 1961 Jun 03, Cairo, Egypt
   b. 1932 Jun 15, Cairo, Egypt
   d. 2012 Dec 24, Virginia Beach, VA
   bur: unk

Attended English school at Heliopolis, Egypt. Spoke fluent English, French, Italian and Arabic. Her first husband was killed in an automobile accident in France as they traveled there on their honeymoon. In the years that followed her recovery from injuries sustained in the accident, she traveled throughout Europe and the United States. In New York, she met U. S. naval officer, Stuart Morgan Beck, who was about to be sent to Egypt to serve as an assistant naval attaché. After his arrival in Egypt, Lola returned to Cairo, at which time they became reacquainted. After some difficulty and delays the two were married in Cairo's Anglican Cathedral adjacent to Tahrir Square. [clxxx]

Children:

4.5005 i.   + Claudia Mountjoy Beck
4.5006 ii.   + Christopher Hollingsworth Beck

4.5005 Claudia Mountjoy 7 Beck *(Stuart6 Evelyn5 George4 Israel3 Sarah 2 Israel1)*

m. Greg Linton Redd, 1986 Sep 16, Arlington, VA

Son of Cecil Redd.

Children:

4.6007 i.   Alexandra Simaika Redd
4.6008 ii.   Jacob Morgan Beck

4.5006 Christopher Hollingsworth 7 Beck *(Stuart6 Evelyn5 George4 Israel3 Sarah 2 Israel1)*

m. Lelia Elizabeth Palmore

Children :

4.6009 i.   Zachariah Fayez Southworth Beck
4.6010 ii.   Madeleine Blanche Beck

4.3003 Catharine Wood 5 Garrard *(George4 Israel3 Sarah 2 Israel1)*
          b. 1898 Dec 15, Frontenac, MN
          d. 1968 Apr 08, Naples, FL
          bur: Old Frontenac Cemetery, Frontenac, MN

          m. Frederic William McMahon, 1923 Jun 23, CA
          b. 1898 Feb 23, New Haven, CT
          d. 1986 Jan 26, Naples, FL
          bur: Arlington National Cemetery, Arlington, VA (Section-8 6060-4-LH)

Son of William John McMahon and May (Reinhardt) McMahon.
Enlisted in the US Navy at age 16; graduated from the US Naval Academy, Annapolis, MD, 1919. At the outbreak of WWII, he held the rank of Lieutenant Commander. During the fighting in the Pacific, he was in command of the aircraft carrier "Suwannee". He later was commander of the carrier "Valley Forge". In 1952, during the Korean conflict, Rear Admiral McMahon was made the Chief of Staff of U. S. Naval Forces in the Far East.

Children:

4.4005 i. + Frederic Garrard McMahon
4.4006 ii. + Georgie Garrard McMahon

4.4005 Frederic Garrard 6 McMahon *(Catharine5 George4 Israel3 Sarah 2 Israel1)*
      b. 1927, FL

"AB, Bowdoin College, 1950;Master of Business Administration, University of
Pennsylvania, 1957. Securities analyst for Merrill Lynch, 1957-1960;
Intermediate analyst Moody's Investor's Service Incorporated, 1960-1968,
senior analyst, 1968-1972, associate director of transportation, 1972-1976,
assistant vice-president, corporate bond research, 1976-1985.
President of Garrard Advisory Corporation."[clxxxi]

      m. Elizabeth Anne Pflug, 1968 Nov 26, Manhasset, NY
      b. 1936, NY

Children:

4.5007 i. Frederic Cole McMahon

4.4006 Georgie Garrard 6 McMahon *(Catharine5 George4 Israel3 Sarah 2 Israel1)*
      b. 1932, VA

      m. Lawrence Maloney Johnson, 1957
      b. 1927 Apr 24, New York City, NY
      d. 1990 Dec 16, Goldens Bridge, NY
      bur: unk

      Son of Leo and Mary Maloney Johnson. "BA, Columbia University;
advertising executive with BBD+O, a Manhattan advertising agency, 1950-1965;
Senior VP of marketing at General Host Corp; president of Comprehensive
Communications; volunteer firefighter for the Scarsdale, NY, fire department
for 26 years; president and member of the Scarsdale Rotary Club."[clxxxii]

Children:

4.5008 i. Mark Johnson
4.5009 ii. Stephen Johnson
4.5010 iii. William Johnson
4.5011 iv. Christopher Johnson
4.5012 v. Lisa Johnson
4.5013 vi. Catherine Johnson

4.1002 Kenner ₃ Garrard *(Sarah 2 Israel 1)*
      b. 1827 Sep 30, "Fairfield", Bourbon Co., KY
      d. 1879 May 15, Cincinnati, OH
      bur: Spring Grove Cemetery, Cincinnati, OH (Section-99 Lot-2)

"Briefly attended Harvard University...but withdrew in his sophomore year after accepting an appointment to the United States Military Academy. He graduated eighth in the Class of 1851 and was appointed a brevet second lieutenant in the 4th U.S. Artillery. He soon transferred to the 1st U.S. Dragoons."[clxxxiii] Stationed in Texas at the outset of the Civil War, Confederate authorities arrested and imprisoned Garrard for his Union loyalty. After his release, he returned east and was appointed colonel of the 146th Infantry in the Army of the Potomac, taking part in the Battles of Fredericksburg, Chancellorsville and Gettysburg. Appointed to command the 2nd Division of Cavalry in the Army of the Cumberland, 1864. He was appointed a brevet major general of volunteers and brevet brigadier general in the regular army. In March of 1865, he was appointed the brevet rank of Major General. Garrard remained in the regular army after the war ended until his resignation in November, 1866. He returned to Cincinnati, working as a real estate broker and Director of the Cincinnati Music Festival. Unmarried/no children.

4.1003 Lewis Hector ₃ Garrard *(Sarah 2 Israel 1)*
      b. 1829 Jun 15, Cincinnati, OH
      d. 1887 Jul 07, Lakewood, NY
      bur: Spring Grove Cemetery, Cincinnati, OH (Section-99 Lot-2)

1853 Graduate of the University of Pennsylvania; member of the Minnesota State Legislature; twice mayor of Lake City, Minnesota.
Author of "Wah-to-yah and the Taos Trail", a book based on his 10 month trek, at age 17, along the Santa Fe Trail from Missouri to New Mexico.[clxxxiv]
He also published the book "Memoir of Charlotte Chambers".

m. Florence Van Vliet, 1862 Oct 25
      b. 1844 Charlotte, VT
      d. 1897 Oct 02, Bellport, NY
      bur: Spring Grove Cemetery, Cincinnati, OH (Section-99 Lot-2)

Children:

4.2004	i.	+ Anna Knapp Garrard	
4.2005	ii.	Winfred Garrard	(1865-1869)
4.2006	iii.	+ Edith Garrard	
4.2007	iv.	Van Vliet Garrard	(1869)

4.2004 Anna Knapp 4 Garrard *(Lewis3 Sarah 2 Israel1)*

> b. 1874 Jun 13, Lake City, MN
> d. 1954 Aug 31, Red Wing, MN
> bur: Evergreen Cemetery, Menominie, WI (Section-2 Lot-74)
>
> m. Paul Carlton Wilson, 1902 Mar 06[clxxxv]
> b. 1869 Feb 15, Reeds Landing, MN
> d. 1950 Nov 14, Red Wing, MN
> bur: Evergreen Cemetery, Menominie, WI (Section-2 Lot-74)
>
> Son of Thomas and Julia (Epley) Wilson.

Children:

4.3004	i.	+	Thomas Blair Wilson
4.3005	ii.	+	Edith Garrard Wilson
4.3006	iii.	+	Lewis Garrard Wilson
4.3007	iv.	+	Julia Frances Wilson
4.3008	v.	+	Mary Blair Wilson

4.3004 Thomas Blair 5 Wilson *(Anna4 Lewis3 Sarah 2 Israel1)*

> b. 1903 Feb 28, Red Cedar, WI
> d. 1975 Aug 24, Anderson, CA
> bur: unk

4.3005 Edith Garrard 5 Wilson *(Anna4 Lewis3 Sarah 2 Israel1)*

> b. 1904 Mar 28, Red Cedar, WI
> d. 1984 Feb 29, Alexandria, VA
> bur: Arlington National Cemetery, Arlington, VA (Section-2 Site-E 248)
>
> m. Newell Dwight Lindner, 1935
> b. 1908 Aug 04, Hempstead, NY
> d. 1961 Aug 08, Falls Church, VA
> bur: Arlington National Cemetery, Arlington, VA (Section-2 Site-E 248)
>
> Son of Paul W. F. Lindner and Margaret Lindner.

Children:

4.4007	i.	Margaret Lindner	b. 1938
4.4008	ii.	Paul C. Lindner	b. 1940

4.3006 Lewis Garrard ₅ Wilson *(Anna4 Lewis3 Sarah 2 Israel1)*
        b. 1905 May 26, Red Cedar, WI
        d. 1987 Sep 28, York, SC
        bur: Rose Hill Cemetery, York, SC (Section-Q)

        m. Wilhemina Lawther Foot
        b. 1912 Dec 20
        d. 1987 Jun 17, SC
        bur: Rose Hill Cemetery, York, SC (Section-Q)

Children:

4.4009 i.   Julia Frances Wilson
4.4010 ii. + Lewis Garrard Wilson, Jr.

4.4010 Lewis Garrard ₆ Wilson, Jr. *(Lewis5 Anna4 Lewis3 Sarah 2 Israel1)*
        b. 1949, SC

        m. Jane Dougherty[clxxxvi]

Children:

4.5014 i.   Daniel Garrard Wilson
4.5015 ii.   Paul Dougherty Wilson

4.3007 Julia Frances ₅ Wilson *(Anna4 Lewis3 Sarah 2 Israel1)*
        b. 1911 Feb 15, WI
        d. 1987 Feb 06
        bur: unk

4.3008 Mary Blair ₅ Wilson *(Anna4 Lewis3 Sarah 2 Israel1)*
        b. 1915, WI
        d. 2005 May 24, Oakmont, PA[clxxxvii]
        bur: Riverview Cemetery, Wabasha, MN

        m. Ralph Sisson Albertson
        b. 1895 May 28, Sioux Falls, SD
        d. 1978 Apr 30, Cable, WI
        bur: Riverview Cemetery, Wabasha, MN

        Son of Charles Albertson and May (Sisson) Albertson.

4.2006 Edith 4 Garrard *(Lewis3 Sarah2 Israel1)*

    b. 1867 Jun 07, Frontenac, MN
    d. 1953 Sep 12, Old Fort, NC
    bur: Evergreen Cemetery, Menominie, WI (Section-2 Lot-76)

    m. Thomas Blair Wilson, Jr. , 1906 Jun 07[clxxxviii]
    b. 1865 Sep 30, Reads Landing, MN
    d. 1936 Oct 04, Menominie, WI
    bur: Evergreen Cemetery, Menominie, WI (Section-2 Lot-76)

    Son of Thomas Blair Wilson and Julia (Epley) Wilson.

Children:

4.3009 i.   Unnamed Infant
4.3010 ii.   + Florence Garrard Wilson

4.3010 Florence Garrard 5 Wilson *(Edith4 Lewis3 Sarah2 Israel1)*

    b. 1909 Oct 10, Menominie, WI
    d. 1978 Dec 21, Naples, FL
    bur: Arlington National Cemetery, Arlington, VA (Section-66 G-2419)

    m. Robert Gardner Baker, 1936 Aug 11
    b. 1910 Nov 21, Spencer, IA
    d. 1979 Aug 01, Naples, FL
    bur: Arlington National Cemetery, Arlington, VA (Section-66 G-2419)

    Son of Guy Gardner Baker and Nina Louise (Larson). Entered West Point, Class of 1934. During WWII, he participated in several European campaigns, earning the Bronze Star, the Croix de Guerre with palm, and a promotion to full colonel. Graduated from the Naval War College in 1948. He then served in Korea, and for his service there, received the Legion of Merit.

Children:

4.4011 i.   Thomas Garrard Baker
4.4012 ii.   + George Gardner Baker
4.4013 iii.   Louisa Baker   (1946-1967)

4.4012 George Gardner 6 Baker *(Florence5 Edith4 Lewis3 Sarah2 Israel1)*

    b. 1943, WI

    m. Jo Anne Marion Christianson, 1971 Aug 14, Ames, IA
    b. 1949. IA

4.1004 Jeptha Dudley 3 Garrard, Jr. *(Sarah 2 Israel 1)*
      b. 1836 Apr 21, Cincinnati, OH
      d. 1915 Dec 16, Cincinnati, OH[clxxxix]
      bur: Spring Grove Cemetery, Cincinnati, OH (Section-99 Lot-2)

He received his preparation for college in Northampton, MA; graduated from Yale in 1858; studied for one year at the Cincinnati Law School, taking the degree of LL.B. in 1859.
"In 1861 Colonel Jeptha Garrard went to New York, and was commissioned a Captain in the Third New York Calvary; promoted to a majorship in the same organization September 27, 1863, and received his commission as Colonel of the First United States Colored Calvary December 7, 1863. He aided in the defense of Washington during the winter of 1861. He saw service with General Banks's army in Northern Virginia the following year and was with Burnside's command in 1862 and 1863. During the remainder of the war his regiment was stationed at Fortress Monroe and at Petersburg, Va. He was breveted a Brigadier General of the volunteer forces on March 13, 1865, and resigned from service April 25, 1865."[cxc]
"He served as president of the Cincinnati Board of Park Commissioners, 1891-1893 and was a member of the Military Order of the Loyal Legion."

      m. Anna Knapp, 1864 Oct
      b. 1840, Auburn, NY
      d. 1887 May 18, Cincinnati, OH
      bur: Spring Grove Cemetery, Cincinnati, OH (Section-99 Lot-2)

Jeptha Dudley Garrard

1836-1915

Photo from the collection of the Ludlow Heritage Museum

John McLean,
Supreme Court Justice

*Photo from the collection of the Ludlow Heritage Museum,
and courtesy of Russell Meyer*

Kenner Garrard
1827-1879
Photo from the collection of the Ludlow Heritage Museum

Israel Garrard
1825-1901
Photo from the collection of the Ludlow Heritage Museum

Frontenac, Minnesota
*Photo from the collection of the Ludlow Heritage Museum,
and courtesy of Russell Meyer*

St. Hubert's Lodge,
Home of Israel Garrard, built 1854,
Frontenac, Minnesota
*Photo from the collection of the Ludlow Heritage Museum,
and courtesy of Russell Meyer*

Israel L. Ludlow Grave Marker
Spring Grove Cemetery
Section 74 Lot 51

Israel L. Ludlow

5.0001   Israel L. 2 Ludlow *(Israel1)*
b. 1804 May 21, Cincinnati, OH
d. 1846 Apr 21, "Elmwood"[cxci], KY[cxcii]
bur: Spring Grove Cemetery, Cincinnati, OH (Section-74 Lot-51)

Israel L. Ludlow was born in May of 1821, four months after his father's death. He was baptized the following month by Rev. James Kemper, the first ordained minister in the Ohio River Valley.[cxciii] Another minister, an associate of Rev. Kemper's, arrived in Cincinnati and was destined to be a part of Israel's upbringing. Rev. David Riske, an Irish-born Presbyterian minister, educated in Scotland, had crossed the Atlantic to serve in a new mission field in America. Charlotte Ludlow married Rev. Riske, and for the next ten years, David Riske was the only father Israel knew, until Rev. Riske's death in 1818. In 1820, Israel's mother took her young family west to Missouri, where she died in 1821.

Thus at age 17, Israel L. Ludlow was left to the guidance of his older brother, James. James brought his brother and younger siblings back from Missouri to Cincinnati.

After their return to Ohio, it was thought by friends and family that an appointment for Israel to the West Point Military Academy in New York may be advantageous. Letters of recommendation were written and sent to the Secretary of War, John C. Calhoun, and arrangements were made for his application.[cxciv]

Israel arrived at West Point in the early summer of 1822 and was admitted to the academy on July 1st. However, over the course of the following months, a list of infractions accumulated in the young cadet's file.[cxcv] Then... "By Orders of December 8, 1822, Cadet Ludlow was arrested and confined for violation of Army Regulations Article 78, Paragraph 98, which states:"Any cadet, who shall play at cards, or any game of chance, shall be dismissed the service, or who shall, without permission, procure or use wine or spirituous liquors, or who shall go to any inn or public house, shall be dismissed the service, or otherwise punished." Ludlow was still present at West Point in January of 1823, but "By Orders of February 8, 1823, Cadet Israel Ludlow, "rejected at the late General Examination," was discharged from the service of the United States effective May 16, 1823. Ludlow's name does not appear on the Muster Roll of the Corps of Cadets after February 1823."[cxcvi]

Israel returned to Cincinnati.

There had arrived in Cincinnati in 1822, cousins from the Chambers side of the family, who had left Maryland to find a new home at Cincinnati. The Cloppers, headed by patriarch Nicholas Clopper, were interested in acquiring land in Texas, but in the meantime, settled into a home in the Mill Creek valley given to them by James Ludlow at Ludlow Station, which they called Beechwood.

By early 1830, Israel was living in boarding house in Cincinnati, when he met Adela Slacum, a new arrival to Cincinnati from Alexandria, Virginia. [cxcvii] Here to visit her older sister, Maria Louisa Benham, Adela extended her stay into the summer months and on June 24th, she and Israel L. Ludlow married.

A long honeymoon trip followed to the Great Lakes, Niagara Falls, New York City and Alexandria, Virginia, before their arrival back in Cincinnati.

In early 1831, a large home and beautiful estate, "Elmwood", located on the Kentucky side of the Ohio River, became available for purchase, and Israel L. Ludlow acquired the property from its owner, William Bullock, formerly of London, England. Bullock had furnished "Elmwood Hall" with European art and furnishings of the highest quality. With the acquisition of the estate, many of these items passed to the ownership of the Ludlow family.

In the spring of that year, the Ludlows had their first child, daughter Louisa, followed by son, George Howard Ludlow the following year in 1832. In all, Israel and Adela would have nine children, losing five of those in early childhood to diseases like Scarlet Fever, 'brain fever" and consumption.

The isolation of Elmwood, proved to be the estate's greatest disadvantage, separating the young family from some of the benefits of society: schools, churches and medical care. [cxcviii]

In 1835, the plight of settlers in Texas in their desire to free themselves from Mexican rule had caused sympathetic Cincinnatians to gather in public meetings to support their cause. A committee was appointed and resolutions were made to provide arms and ammunition to the settlers. Israel was one of five members appointed to the committee and Nicholas Clopper served as the chairman. [cxcix] The group adopted a resolution to provide weapons to Texas. For Israel's role in smuggling two cannons, along with powder and shot, he was sued by the State of Ohio. [cc]

Determined to leave Elmwood and to settle in Texas, Israel sold Elmwood Hall to brother-in-law George Kenner in 1840 and moved his family into a house elsewhere on the estate which became known as the "Ludlow Homestead".

In early 1842, he traveled to the area of Matagorda Bay along the Gulf Coast and soon acquired a large tract of land there along Caney Creek. The transaction involved an exchange of land as Israel Ludlow came into possession of the property of Elias Wightman, while Wightman received the Elmwood acreage. [cci] Ludlow also entered into a partnership with Samuel Patterson who would manage the Caney Creek property. Ludlow returned to Kentucky and brought his family to their new home in Texas. Their residence in Texas was of short duration. A series of unfortunate events, which included the sudden and unexpected deaths of both Patterson and Wightman, caused the Ludlow family to leave Texas and return to Elmwood. [ccii]

The widow of Elias Wightman contested the terms of the agreement that had been made between her husband and Israel Ludlow. As a result, Mary Wightman received a monetary settlement and Israel Ludlow retained ownership of both properties.

In 1845, deep in debt and with his health declining, Israel wrote his will...

"In the name of God, Amen.

I, Israel L. Ludlow of the County of Kenton and Commonwealth of Kentucky, being of infirm health yet of sound and disposing memory and remembering the frailty of human life, feel deeply impressed with gratitude to my Heavenly Father for sustaining me thus long and likewise feel it my imperative duty to settle (as far as I can) my worldly affairs, and to dispose of such goods of this as the Lord in his goodness and mercy has bestowed upon me, for which purpose I do ordain, make and publish this my last Will and Testament..." The document named Adela as his sole beneficiary and executrix of his estate, and instructed that the Texas property be sold..."*excepting my slaves which are not to be sold in any event"*. *"It is my further will that all the slaves in Texas belonging to me...be emancipated...and brought here at the expense of my estate, taking from them a written obligation to serve for the term of five years from their arrival"*. Further instructions in the document were to sell parts of the Elmwood farm, while providing free land for the establishment of churches in the community. For his children, Israel's will provided an amount of $1250 to each child at the age of 21, but adding *"my wish is that they shall be enabled to enter life free from the withering blight of debt, and that my dear wife should often endeavor to instill into their minds the direful consequences always attending the habit of contracting debts"*. [cciii]

In April, 1846, the Cincinnati Daily Gazette published the following notice...

"Died,

At his residence in Kenton county, Kentucky, of consumption, on the evening of the 21st inst., ISRAEL L. LUDLOW, aged 40 years.

Mr. Ludlow was a native of this county, the youngest son of the late Col. Ludlow. He had been afflicted with the disease of which he died for several years, but he rode out on the day of his death, and appeared easy. While conversing with friends, the sudden rupture of a blood vessel caused his death in a very short time.

The funeral procession will move at 3 ½ o'clock, P. M., this day, from Ludlow's ferry, to the Presbyterian burying ground in this city." [cciv]

Within a year, the Texas property had been sold to George Kenner. Over time, the Ludlow estate was subdivided and the lots were sold or auctioned. A community was formed, known as "Elmwood", until February of 1864, when the village was incorporated as the town of Ludlow, Kentucky, named to honor Israel L. Ludlow and the Ludlow family. [ccv]

m. Helen Adela Slacum, 1830 Jun 24, Cincinnati, OH
b. 1807 Jul 23, Alexandria, VA[ccvi]
d. 1872 Mar 05, Ludlow, KY[ccvii]
bur: Spring Grove Cemetery, Cincinnati, OH (Section-74 Lot-51)

In 1831, Israel and Adela moved into Elmwood Hall, a large and beautiful residence within view of the Ohio River.[ccviii]

During their years at Elmwood, Adela became the mother of nine children, but she lost five of them to childhood illness and disease.

By the time of Israel's death in 1846, the Ludlows had left Elmwood Hall and were living in another residence on the property, the Ludlow Homestead.

Adela encountered some resentment from her Elmwood neighbors, due to her Virginia upbringing. Few southerners lived in the community, prior to and during the Civil War years. Adela, as the most prominent southerner in their midst, was referred to as 'the old secession woman" and was resented by some for her southern sympathies.[ccix]

In November of 1863, two unexpected visitors arrived at the front door of the Ludlow Homestead. These were Confederate General John Hunt Morgan and Captain Thomas Hines, who had escaped from a Columbus, Ohio, prison and boarded a train southward to Cincinnati....

"...Instead , then, of going to the depot in Cincinnati, we got off, while the train was moving slowly, in the outskirts of the city, near Ludlow Ferry, on the Ohio River. Going directly to the ferry we were crossed over in a skiff and landed immediately in front of the residence of Mrs. Ludlow. We rang the door-bell, a servant came, and General Morgan wrote upon a visiting-card, "General Morgan and Captain Hines, escaped." We were warmly received, took a cup of coffee with the family, were furnished a guide, and walked some three miles in the country, where we were furnished horses." [ccx]

The South celebrated Morgan's escape, and those who had assisted him along the way.

Adela Ludlow's death occurred at the Ludlow Homestead on March 5, 1872. Her funeral was held at her church, Trinity Episcopal, in Covington.

Children:

5.1001	i.	+ Louisa Adela Ludlow	
5.1002	ii.	+ George Howard Ludlow	
5.1003	iii.	Jane Ludlow	(1834-1838)
5.1004	iv.	James Chambers Ludlow	(1836-1838)
5.1005	v.	Henry Spencer Ludlow	(1837-1841)
5.1006	vi.	Adela Ludlow	(1839)
5.1007	vii.	+ William Slacum Ludlow	
5.1008	viii.	+ Albert Sloo Ludlow	
5.1009	ix.	Worcester Ludlow	(1846)[ccxi]

5.1001 Louisa Adela ₃ Ludlow *(Israel2 Israel1)*

  b. 1831 Mar 27, Cincinnati, OH

  d. 1885 Apr 27, Ludlow, KY[ccxii]

  bur: Spring Grove Cemetery, Cincinnati, OH (Section-74 Lot-51)

"Of the [Ludlow] children Louisa was the eldest. The good people who knew her from childhood to the grave say that she was a bright child and a noble, charitably disposed and fine looking woman." [ccxiii]

Louisa Ludlow was married first to William Goodloe, a young war veteran who had just recently returned from the battlefields of Mexico. Goodloe's father, James, had purchased Elmwood Hall, the former Ludlow family home, and the young couple lived there with his parents.[ccxiv] Two daughters, Helen and Georgia, were born to their union but, by 1853, marital difficulties prompted Louisa to petition for a divorce. William abandoned the family and left the area for parts unknown.[ccxv]

In October of 1854, Louisa married William Hubbard Mitchell III, of Richmond, Virginia. Louisa returned with him to settle there, leaving Helen and Georgia behind to live with her mother, Adela. William and Louisa Mitchell became the parents of two daughters of their own, but in October of 1861, William died, and their two daughters died shortly thereafter.

A month after the death of Mr. Mitchell, Louisa married her third husband, William Barnet Phillips. As with her previous marriages, this too was of short duration.[ccxvi]

In the closing months of the Civil War, Louisa was "stranded in Richmond, prompting Adela Ludlow to ask [Salmon P.] Chase to arrange authorization for Louisa's return north through military lines."[ccxvii] Louisa received the necessary papers and fled northward to New York City, apparently just in time to escape the flames that burned Richmond in April of 1865.

By the spring of 1868, Louisa was back at "Elmwood"[ccxviii] to marry her fourth husband, Edward Westcott, of Hartford, Connecticut. The newlyweds took up residence afterward in Hartford, taking Louisa's daughters, Helen and Georgia with them. Difficulties arose in their marriage and, once again, Louisa's marriage ended in divorce.[ccxix]

After her mother died in 1872, Louisa demanded a division of the family property. In the years that followed, Louisa accused her brothers of keeping the most valuable land for themselves, assigning to her the remainder. By 1882, Louisa had left New England, returned to Kentucky and built a large brick residence on her riverfront property. She then promptly took her brothers to court, accompanied by her fifth husband, Edward H. Maxwell of Boston. [ccxx]

Newspapers covered the courtroom drama as the family feud unfolded. The proceedings included "lively exchanges of dirt-slinging" but the final result was the vindication of William and Albert Ludlow. Not long afterward Louisa died at her Ludlow, Kentucky residence and was buried at Spring Grove. [ccxxi]

m1 William H. H. Goodloe, ca. 1850 (div. ca 1853)
b. ca.1825, OH
d. unk
bur: unk

Son of James and Miriam (Weaver) Goodloe.[ccxxii] Served in Capt. Samuel Walker's Texas Rangers. During the War with Mexico he served as 2nd Lt. of Co. B, 15th Ohio Infantry and was wounded at the Battle of Churubusco.[ccxxiii]
In 1847 he was assigned to the Newport Barracks at Newport, Kentucky.[ccxxiv]

m2 William Hubbard Mitchell III, 1854 Oct 03, "Elmwood", KY[ccxxv]
b. 1828 Oct 26, Richmond, VA
d. 1861 Oct 06, Williamsburg, VA[ccxxvi]
bur: Hollywood Cemetery, Richmond, VA (Section-K Lot-99)

Son of William H. Mitchell, Jr. and Julia Ann (Burnham) Mitchell.[ccxxvii] Attended William and Mary College.[ccxxviii] Bookkeeper/Accountant.[ccxxix]

m3 William Barnet Phillips, 1861 Nov 07, Richmond, VA[ccxxx]

m4 Edward Gardiner Westcott, 1868 Apr 29, Ludlow, KY (div. 1873)[ccxxxi]
b. 1831 Jul 07, Davenport, NY
d. 1897 Dec 31, Hartford, CT
bur: Cedar Grove Cemetery, New London, CT (Section-21 Lot-3)

Son of Dr. Gardiner Westcott and Mary Anne (Dent).

m5 Edward H. Maxwell, 1874 May 21, Portland, ME
b. ca. 1849, Boston, MA
d. 1894 Jul 10, Watertown, MA
bur: Wyoming Cemetery, Melrose, MA (Pine Avenue Lot-779)

Son of Edward Maxwell and Nancy (Boardman).

Children (m1);

| 5.2001 | i. | + | Helen Adela Goodloe | |
| 5.2002 | ii. | + | Georgia Goodloe | |

Children (m2):

| 5.2003 | iii. | Louisa "Loulie" Mitchell | (1857-1863) |
| 5.2004 | iv. | Rosalie Mitchell | (1858-1861)[ccxxxii] |

5.2001 Helen Adela 4 Goodloe* *(Louise3 Israel2 Israel1)*
      b. 1850 Oct 20, Ludlow, KY
      d. 1910 Mar 19, Boston, MA
      bur: Spring Grove Cemetery, Cincinnati, OH (Section-74 Lot-51)

*After her mother's marriage to her second husband, Wm. Mitchell, in 1854, Helen was adopted by him and used the surname Mitchell.

      m. James Thompson Bryant (div. 1894[ccxxxiii])
      b. 1844 May 03, Barre, MA
      d. 1918 Feb 11, Boston, MA[ccxxxiv]
      bur: Lincoln Cemetery, Barre, MA

      Son of Walter A. and Lydia (Thompson) Bryant.

Children:

5.3001 i.   + Louise Ludlow Bryant
5.3002 ii. + Lydia Thompson Bryant

5.3001 Louise Ludlow 5 Bryant *(Helen4 Louise3 Israel2 Israel1)*
      b. 1873 Jun 14, Worcester, MA
      d. 1926 Nov 03, Boston, MA
      bur: Mt. Auburn Cemetery, Cambridge, MA

      m1 Frederick Nash Read, ca. 1894 (div.)
      b. 1872 Aug , "Eagle Point", Mecklenberg Co., VA
      d. 1959, Feb 05, Sarasota, FL
      bur: Sarasota Memorial Park Cemetary, Sarasota, FL

      Son of Edmund (Strudwick) and Mary (Morton Sturdivant) Read.

      m2 Joseph Irving Estes
      b. 1855 Sep 13, East Abington, MA
      d. 1924 Mar 11, Boston, MA
      bur: Mt. Auburn Cemetery, Cambridge, MA

      Son of Joseph and Mary (Torrey) Estes.

Children (m1):

5.4001 i.   + Dorothy Louise Read

5.4001 Dorothy Louise 6 Read *(Louise5 Helen4 Louise3 Israel2 Israel1)*
b. 1896 Mar 10, Ludlow, KY
d. 1974 Mar 14, Los Angeles, CA
bur: unk

m1 Erich Rudolph Volkmann, 1917 Aug 18, Boston, MA
b. 1890 Jun 11, Dusseldorf, Germany
d. 1970 Dec 08, Santa Barbara, CA
bur: unk

Son of Heinrich Volkmann.

m2 Edward Abbott, 1973, Santa Barbara, CA

Children(m1):

5.5001 i.	Erich Rudolph Volkmann, Jr.	(1918-1978)
5.5002 ii.	Robert Bryant Volkmann	(1921-1975)
5.5003 iii. +	Sylvia Dorothy Volkmann	

5.5003 Sylvia Dorothy 7 Volkmann *(Dorothy6 Louise5 Helen4 Louise3 Israel2 Israel1)*
b. 1925, RI

m1 Paul Michael Brickley, 1950 January 21, St. Paul, MN
b. 1917 Nov 22, Two Harbors, MN
d. 1962 Jan 30, Santa Barbara, CA
bur: Santa Barbara Cemetery, Santa Barbara, CA (Ocean View G-126)

Son of Michael and Elizabeth (Bagnell) Brickley.
"Graduate of the University of Michigan; attended Medical School at the University of Minnesota; interned at St. Luke's Hospital, Chicago, IL. During WWII he was an Army Captain posted at Gorgas Hospital in Panama. After the war, he joined the Ophthalmology Department at the Mayo Clinic in Rochester, MN, and following his residency was appointed to the Staff. In 1954, he and his family moved to Santa Barbara, CA, where he joined the Sansum Clinic. He was active in several community organizations and volunteer medical outreach services, as well as social clubs and All Saints Episcopal Church."

m2 LeRoy Ashton Weller, Jr., 1990 Nov 03, Carpinteria, CA
b. 1921 Mar 15, Cucamonga, CA
d. 2000 Apr 11, Carpinteria, CA
bur: c/ ashes scattered

Son of LeRoy Ashton Weller, Sr. and Emily (Highley).

Children (m1):

5.6001 i.   +   Mark Paul Brickley
5.6002 ii.   +   Elizabeth Read Brickley
5.6003 iii   Julia Louise Brickley   (1957-1959)

5.6001 Mark Paul 8 Brickley *(Sylvia7 Dorothy6 Louise5 Helen4 Louise3 Israel2 Israel1)*
b. 1951, MN

5.6002 Elizabeth Read 8 Brickley *(Sylvia7 Dorothy6 Louise5 Helen4 Louise3 Israel2 Israel1)*
b.1953, MN

m. Patrick Timothy Adams, 1989 Apr 23, Sausalito, CA
b. 1953, CA

Son of William Adams and Settie (Retherford) Adams.

Children:

5.7001 i.   Jackson Nash Adams   b. 1991, CA
5.7002 ii.   Russell Sturdivant Adams   b. 1993, CA

5.3002 Lydia Thompson 5 Bryant *(Helen4 Louise3 Israel2 Israel1)*
b. 1877 Jun 14, Worcester, MA
d. 1949 Sep 20, Santa Barbara, CA[ccxxxv]
bur: c

m1 Bertram Grosvenor Goodhue, 1902 Apr 08, Boston, MA
b. 1869 Apr 28, Pomfret, CT
d. 1924 Apr 23, New York, NY
bur: Chapel of the Intercession, New York City, NY

Son of Charles and Helen Grosvenor Eldredge Goodhue. He attended Russell's Collegiate and Commercial Institute. Although he did not attend a university, he received an honorary degree from Trinity College in Connecticut in 1911. In 1884 he moved to New York City to apprentice in the architectural firm of Renwick, Aspinwall and Russell. His apprenticeship ended in 1891 and he moved to Boston, where he formed a business partnership with Ralph Adams Cram that lasted almost 25 years.   The firm was a leader in Neo-Gothic architecture. Goodhue left in 1914 and began his own firm, moving into other architectural styles such as Byzantine Revival and Spanish Colonial Revival. His sudden death in 1924 marked the end of a brilliant career and the loss of a man much admired by his peers.

Some of his most notable designs included:

- The United States Military Academy Chapel, West Point, NY, 1906
- El Fureidis, Montecito, CA, 1906
- Saint Thomas Church, New York City, NY, 1906
- Church of the Intercession, New York City, NY, 1913
- Virginia Military Institute, Lexington, VA, 1914
- Los Angeles Central Library, Los Angeles, CA, 1924
- Nebraska State Capitol, Lincoln, NE, 1924
- National Academy of Sciences Building, Washington, DC, 1924

m2 Hannibal Ingalls Kimball, 1929 Jul 25, Stroudsburg, PA
   b. 1874 Apr 02, Newton, MA
   d. 1933 Oct 16, Mount McGregor, NY[ccxxxvi]
   bur: Green-wood Cemetery, Brooklyn, NY (Section-146 Lot-25299)

Son of Hannibal, Sr. and Mary (Cook) Kimball. Entered Harvard University at the age of 16, Class of 1894. Junior member of Stone & Kimball Publishing Co. and chief executive of Cheltenham Press.[ccxxxvii]

Children(m1):

5.4002 i.   + Frances Bertram Goodhue
5.4003 ii. + Hugh Grosvenor Bryant Goodhue

5.4002 Frances Bertram 6 Goodhue *(Lydia5 Helen4 Louise3 Israel2 Israel1)*
   b. 1904 Apr 11, New York, NY
   d. 1989 Apr 12, Santa Barbara, CA
   bur: c

   m. Henry Yates Satterlee, 1925 Jun 08, New York, NY[ccxxxviii]
   b. 1900 Apr 08, Morgantown, NC
   d. 1977 Sep 29, Burbank, CA
   bur: Forest Lawn Memorial Park, Hollywood Hills, CA

Son of Rev. Churchill and Helen Stuyvesant (Folsom) Satterlee.

Children:

5.5004 i.   + Lydia Goodhue Satterlee
5.5005 ii.   Helen Stuyvesant Satterlee   (1930)
5.5006 iii. + Frances Yates Satterlee
5.5007 iv.   + Henry Yates Satterlee, Jr.

5.5004 Lydia Goodhue 7 Satterlee *(Frances6 Lydia5 Helen4 Louise3 Israel2 Israel1)*
      b. 1926 Oct 23, Morristown, NJ
      d. 1992 Jul 02, Bar Harbor, ME
      bur: Forest Hill Cemetery, Northeast Harbor, ME

      m. Henry Channing Rivers, 1948 Dec 17, Solvang, CA
      b. 1917 May 06, Wellesley, MA
      d. 1996 Dec 21, Northeast Harbor, ME[ccxxxix]
      bur: Forest Hill Cemetery, Northeast Harbor, ME

      Son of Robert Wheaton and Rosalie (Channing) Rivers. Studied at the Rivers School, Boston, which his father had founded; the Deane School; and the School of the Arts, Santa Barbara, California. Artist and poet; involved in architectural and landscape design.

Children:

5.6004 i.   John Russell Rivers
5.6005 ii.   Ann Goodhue Rivers

5.6004 John Russell 8 Rivers *(Lydia7 Frances6 Lydia5 Helen4 Louise3 Israel2 Israel1)*
      b. 1950, CA

Architect and photographer.

      m. Carol Lynn Beardsley, 1971 Jun 05, Auburn, NY
      b.1950, NY

Children:

5.7003 i.   + Ann Elizabeth Rivers

5.6005 Ann Goodhue 8 Rivers *(Lydia7 Frances6 Lydia5 Helen4 Louise3 Israel2 Israel1)*
      b. 1955

      m. Stephen J. Mullane, 1984 May 30, Bar Harbor, ME (div.)

Children:

5.7004 i.   + Benjamin Alden Rivers Mullane
5,7005 ii.   Anthony Ross Rivers Mullane

5.7004 Benjamin Alden Rivers 9 Mullane *(Ann8 Lydia7 Frances6 Lydia5 Helen4 Louise3 Israel2 Israel1)*
        b. 1986, ME

5.5006 Frances Yates "Fay" 7 Satterlee *(Frances6 Lydia5 Helen4 Louise3 Israel2 Israel1)*
        b. 1931, NY

        m. Grant Owen Engle, 1951 Feb 16, Los Angeles, CA
        b. 1929 Feb 24, WA
        d. 2002 Jun 19, Los Angeles, CA
        bur: c

        Son of Albert Grant Engle and Viva Pearl (Wittel).

Children:

5.6006 i.   + Eric Owen Engle

5.6006 Eric Owen 8 Engle *(Frances7 Frances6 Lydia5 Helen4 Louise3 Israel2 Israel1)*
        b. 1952, CA

        m. Adele Fong, 1977 May 28, Los Angeles, CA
        b. 1951, Tahiti

Children:

5.7005 i.   + Kimberly Tiare Engle
5.7006 ii.   David Heimana Engle   b. 1980, CA
5.7007 iii.   Gregory Engle   b. 1982, CA

5.7005 Kimberly Tiare 9 Engle *(Eric8 Frances7 Frances6 Lydia5 Helen4 Louise3 Israel2 Israel1)*
        b. 1979, CA

        m. Gregory Howard

Children:

5.8001 i.   Evan Theodore Owen Howard   b. 2015, CA

5.5007 Henry Yates 7 Satterlee, Jr. *(Frances6 Lydia5 Helen4 Louise3 Israel2 Israel1)*

b. 1935, NY

m1 Arlene Schroeder, 1960 Mar 25, Santa Barbara, CA (div. 1983)
b. 1937, OH

m2 Maria Teresa Olivera Elizalde, 2002 Oct 05, Santa Barbara, CA
b. 1947, Mexico

Children(m1):

5.6007 i.   + Christopher Yates Satterlee
5.6008 ii.   + Lydia Goodhue Satterlee
5.6009 iii.   + Rachel Lynn Satterlee

5.6007 Christopher Yates 8 Satterlee *(Henry7 Frances6 Lydia5 Helen4 Louise3 Israel2 Israel1)*

b. 1960, CA

m. Carol Mutsuye Yamane, 1987 Apr 04, Stamford, CT
b. 1957, CA

Children:

5.7008 i.	Allison Chisako Satterlee	b. 1989, CA
5.7009 ii.	Ryan Yates Tetsuo Satterlee	b. 1991, CA

5.6008 Lydia Goodhue 8 Satterlee *(Henry7 Frances6 Lydia5 Helen4 Louise3 Israel2 Israel1)*

b. 1962, CA

m1 John F. Roskoski, 1983 May 21, Santa Barbara, CA (div.1998)
b. 1950, CA

m2 John Weaver Lawson, 2001 May 05,
b. 1961, CA

Children(m2):

5.8002 i.	Christopher James Lawson	b. 2002

5.6009 Rachel Lynn 8 Satterlee *(Henry7 Frances6 Lydia5 Helen4 Louise3 Israel2 Israel1)*

b. 1968, CA

m. Colin Mark Zak, 1992 Aug 30
b. 1967, CA

Children:

5.7010 i.   Avery Anna Zak   b. 1999, CA
5.7011 ii.   Jaiden Andrew Zak   b. 2001, CA

5.4003 Hugh Grosvenor Bryant 6 Goodhue *(Lydia5 Helen4 Louise3 Israel2 Israel1)*
b. 1905 Apr 29, New York, NY
d. 1989 Aug 08, Pasadena, CA
bur: c

m. Grace Irwin "Fanny" Bright, 1938 Apr 26, Baltimore, MD
b. 1913 Nov 15, Philadelphia, PA
d. 2000 Dec 15, Los Angeles, CA
bur: c

Children:

5.5007 i.   + Nicholas Bright Goodhue
5.5008 ii.   + Jill Putnam Goodhue

5.5007 Nicholas Bright 7 Goodhue *(Hugh6 Lydia5 Helen4 Louise3 Israel2 Israel1)*
b. 1942, CA

Graduated from Williams College in 1964 with a B.A. in Latin; M.A. in Latin at UCLA, 1968; J.D. at the UCLA School of Law, 1979. Became a freelance researcher and manuscript editor.
Author of "The Lucus Furrinae and the Syrian Sanctuary on the Janiculum" (Amsterdam: Adolf M Hakkert, 1975) and several articles in the field of classical archaeology.

5.5008 Jill Putnam 7 Goodhue *(Hugh6 Lydia5 Helen4 Louise3 Israel2 Israel1)*
b. 1945, CA

m. Gerben Hoeksma, 1973 Apr 07, Pasadena, CA
b. 1947, CA

Children:

5.6010 i.   + Nicole Goodhue Hoeksma
5.6011 ii.   Anne Bright Hoeksma   b. 1983, CA

5.6010 Nicole Goodhue 8 Hoeksma *(Jill7 Hugh6 Lydia5 Helen4 Louise3 Israel2 Israel1)*
> b. 1979

> m. Christopher Gerald Gordon, 2009 July 11, Ojai, CA

Children:

5.7012 i.   Goldie Goodhue Gordon   b. 2013

5.2002 Georgia 4 Goodloe[ccxl] *(Louise3 Israel2 Israel1)*
> b. 1853, OH
> d. 1925 Jan 25, Chicago, IL
> bur: Spring Grove Cemetery, Cincinnati, OH (Section-74- Lot-51)

Raised by her grandmother in Kentucky, Georgia moved with her mother and step-father, Edward Westcott, to Hartford, CT, in 1868, but the relationship between daughter and mother seems to have always been a difficult one. Georgia ran away from home; associated herself with people and places considered to be of poor reputation; and, at least once, was committed by her mother to an asylum.[ccxli] Louisa removed Georgia from her will, other than arranging for a small allowance. After her mother's death, Georgia contested the will, and won, being awarded half of her mother's inheritance.[ccxlii] However, the other result of the legal proceedings was the revelation of Georgia's scandalous past, which was publicly exposed during court testimony, and repeated through newspaper accounts from the trial.[ccxliii]

> m. Thomas L. Connor, New York City, NY[ccxliv]
> b. ----
> d. 187-, Georgetown, CA
> bur: unk

"A leading man in a theatrical company". No children.

5.1002 George Howard 3 Ludlow *(Israel2 Israel1)*
> b. 1832 Jul 25, "Elmwood" (Ludlow), KY
> d. 1853 Aug 04, Lake Erie
> bur: Spring Grove Cemetery, Cincinnati, OH (Section-74 Lot-51)

As the oldest son, he was in line to receive the major portion of the family inheritance and, undoubtedly, was educated and prepared for the responsibility of managing the family estate. His sudden and untimely death at age 21, aboard the ship "Crescent City", on Lake Erie, en route from Cleveland, Ohio, to Buffalo, New York, was attributed to "disease of the heart".[ccxlv]

5.1007   William Slacum "Will" 3 Ludlow *(Israel2 Israel1)*
        b. 1841 Feb 15, Louisville, KY
        d. 1931 Jul 30, Cincinnati, OH[ccxlvi]
        bur: Spring Grove Cemetery, Cincinnati, OH (Section-74 Lot-51)

He was born in Louisville, Kentucky, at the home of George Dennison Prentice, the famed editor of the Louisville Journal[ccxlvii].
"Educated in the public schools of Cincinnati, Mr. Ludlow later was graduated from Miami University."[ccxlviii]
He graduated from Cincinnati Law School in 1866, and admitted to the Ohio State Bar that same year.
He lived in Ludlow, Kentucky, until about 1875, when he moved across the river to Cincinnati, residing there the remainder of his life.
One source, from 1892, listed his occupation and address, at that time, as a "Real Estate Broker. Address, 77 Garfield Place [Cincinnati]."[ccxlix]
He was instrumental in the growth and development of the town of Ludlow, Kentucky. In the 1870's, he assisted in bringing the Cincinnati Southern Railroad through Ludlow by leasing family property for their use.[ccl] Even in later years, when the railroad began bypassing smaller towns along its route, the Southern always stopped at the Ludlow depot, as long as a passenger train went through town. This was due to a requirement that William Ludlow placed in the lease agreement with the railroad.
William Ludlow also provided land on the western edge of town for a large amusement park called the Ludlow Lagoon, which opened in 1895.
By 1904, William Ludlow was the president of the Lagoon Company[ccli]
At that time, he was living at the Alta Building, Fourth and Sycamore streets, where he lived until 1919. That February, Ludlow, a "retired capitalist and former prominent Cincinnati attorney, was shot and seriously wounded by two men who entered his apartments on the fifth floor of the Alta Building."[cclii]
Although severely injured in the failed robbery attempt, he survived, and moved into the Lombardy Building at 332 West Fourth Street.
William Ludlow died twelve years later, in 1931, from the "infirmities of age".
In his later years, not only had he been shot but also twice hit by automobiles and still lived to the age of 90 years old.
He was known as a historian, a student of literature and as a collector of books, many of them first editions of great value.
The funeral was held at Christ Episcopal Church in Cincinnati.
William Ludlow never married. Many of the books from his personal collection were donated to the library of the University of Cincinnati. His papers, journals and letters are in the collection of the Cincinnati Historical Society.
Paintings and family portraits; real estate and other possessions were divided among William's niece and nephews, Albert's children.

5.1008 Albert Sloo 3 Ludlow *(Israel2 Israel1)*

> b. 1844 May --, "Elmwood" (Ludlow), KY
> d. 1919 Oct 05, Milwaukee, WI[ccliii]
> bur: Prairie Home Cemetery, Waukesha, WI (Section-G Block-62 Lot-2)

Attended schools in Covington, Kentucky; Cincinnati, Ohio; and Miami University, Oxford, Ohio. During the Civil War he was commissioned as an Ensign and assigned to the U.S. Flagship Black Hawk of the Mississippi Squadron, based at Mound City, Illinois. He served under the command of Admirals David Dixon Porter and Samuel Phillips Lee. It was at Mound City that Albert married his first wife, Sarah "Sallie" Friganza.[ccliv]

He was honorably discharged on the 20th of July, 1868, and he and Sallie left Illinois to live at the "Ludlow Homestead" in Ludlow, Kentucky, raising their children there. Albert was actively involved in community matters, serving as city alderman, 1869-1875; assisting in organizing a Ludlow baseball team and helping to establish a volunteer fire department for the town.[cclv]

In September of 1874, Albert travelled north to the states of Illinois, Minnesota and Wisconsin, and in the following year, he and his family moved to Waukesha, Wisconsin. The area there was well-known for its "Bethesda Waters", a natural water revered for its medicinal properties, and Albert cited health concerns as his motivation for the move.[cclvi]

Almost immediately after the move, Albert and Sarah separated and filed for divorce. The ensuing court proceedings included accusations of infidelity and abandonment, resulting in Albert having custody of the children.[cclvii]

Albert married second Laura deRushe, described as a "handsome brunette and a brilliant woman".[cclviii] In addition to raising the two children from Albert's first marriage, the couple became parents to three children of their own.

In Waukesha, Albert became prominent in the community.

The Ludlow home, at 401 Maple Street, became a gathering place for local society, and he and Laura hosted numerous parties and events there. The residence was noted in newspapers and among the citizenry as housing one of the finest private art collections of the Midwest.[cclix]

In 1888, Albert served as a delegate to the Republican Convention in Chicago.[cclx]

In February of 1897, Laura died, and the following October Albert married Margaret deRushe, Laura's niece.

Over the years, Albert retained close friendships and associations with actor Joseph Jefferson; author Eugene Field; and his crewmates from the USS Black Hawk. He served as a commander of the Loyal Legion for the state of Wisconsin and was a devoted member of St. Matthias Episcopal Church of Waukesha.

He died in Milwaukee in October of 1919.[cclxi]

m1 Sarah "Sallie" Friganza, 1868 Apr 04, Mound City, IL (div., 1877)[cclxii]
b. 1848, NY
d. 1893 Nov 07, Chicago, IL
bur: unk

m2 Laura deRushe, 1877 Sep 06, Dayton, OH
b. 1853 Nov 27, Lewisburg, OH
d. 1897 Feb 11, Waukesha, WI[cclxiii]
bur: Prairie Home Cemetery, Waukesha, WI (Section-G Block-62 Lot-2)

m3 Margaret deRushe, 1897 Oct 06, Darke Co., OH[cclxiv]
b. 1869 Jul 31, Greenville, OH
d. 1933 Jul 30, Waukesha,WI
bur: Prairie Home Cemetery, Waukesha, WI (Section-G Block-62 Lot-2)

Children (m1):

5.2005	i.	Adela Slacum Ludlow	(1868-1943)
5.2006	ii.	+ William Albert Ludlow	

Children (m2):

5.2007	iii.	+ Leo deRushe Ludlow	
5.2008	iv.	Reginald Fairfax "Rex"Ludlow	(1883-1913)[cclxv]
5.2009	v.	+ Frederick Hubert Israel Ludlow	

5.2006 William Albert 4 Ludlow *(Albert3 Israel2 Israel1)*
b. 1873 Jul 03, Ludlow, KY
d. 1957 Mar 26, Los Angeles, CA
bur: Prairie Home Cemetery, Waukesha, WI (Section-G Block-62 Lot-2)

m. Julia Cohn, 1910 Feb 05, Chicago, IL
b. 1878 Dec --, Jackson, MI
d. 1949 Jan 04, Los Angeles, CA
bur: Prairie Home Cemetery, Waukesha, WI (Section-G Block-62 Lot-2)

Children:

5.3003	i.	+ William Albert Ludlow, Jr.
5.3004	ii.	+ Jane Ludlow

5.3003 William Albert 5 Ludlow, Jr. *(William4 Albert3 Israel2 Israel1)*
   b. 1911 Jul 07, Chicago, IL
   d. 1975 Dec 29, Pasadena, CA
   bur: Mountain View Cemetery, Pasadena, CA

   m. Lydia Augusta Jaenke, 1943 Dec 25, Pasadena, CA
   b. 1911 Jan 27, Ludington, WI
   d. 2000 Sep 28, Portland, OR
   bur: unk

5.3004 Jane 5 Ludlow *(William4 Albert3 Israel2 Israel1)*
   b. 1918 Jun 12, Chicago, IL
   d. 1999 Nov 21, Carson City, NV
   bur: c

   m1 Parker

   m2 Wilfred Kenneth Blackburn
   b. 1916 Aug 30, Los Angeles, CA
   d. 1999 Jun 15, Sagle, ID
   bur: c

   Son of Hugh Arnold McVicar Blackburn and Lulu (Davenport).

Children(m1):

5.4004 i.   Philip Parker

Children(m2):

5.4005 ii.   + Anita Ludlow Blackburn

5.4005 Anita Ludlow 6 Blackburn *(Jane5 William4 Albert3 Israel2 Israel1)*
   b. 1949, CA

   m1 Terry Lee Potter
   m2 Richard Truesdell
   m3 Leon Treants, 1992 Sep 19, Carson City, NV

Children (m1):

5.5009 i.   + Terry Thomas Potter

5.5009 Terry Thomas ₇ Potter *(Anita6 Jane5 William4 Albert3 Israel2 Israel1)*
      b. 1970

Served in the 82nd Airborne Division during the Persian Gulf War, 1990-1991.

      m. Laura Fleger

Children:

5.6012 i.   Justin Rae Thomas Potter   b. 1996

5.2007 Leo deRushe ₄ Ludlow *(Albert3 Israel2 Israel1)*
      b. 1879 Oct 06, Waukesha, WI
      d. 1941 Mar 03, Tulsa, OK[cclxvi]
      bur: Tulsa Memorial Park, Tulsa, OK (Section-42 Lot-14)

"Graduate of the University of Wisconsin, he received his law degree at the University of Chicago. Employee of the legal department for the Tidal Oil company and later formed his own oil lease and production concern."[cclxvii]

      m. Jane Alexander, 1917 May 17, Tulsa, OK[cclxviii]
      b. 1892 May 03, Harmony, PA
      d. 1966 Jul 17, Beverly Hills, CA
      bur: c

Children:

5.3005 i.   + John deRushe Ludlow

5.3005 John deRushe "Jack" ₅ Ludlow *(Leo4 Albert3 Israel2 Israel1)*
      b. 1918 Apr 09, Tulsa, OK
      d. 1984 Dec 15, Costa Mesa, CA
      bur: c

Attended schools in Tulsa, Oklahoma; Culver Military Institute, Culver, Indiana; graduate of Miami University, Oxford, Ohio. Served as a pilot during WWII in North Africa and was awarded several medals of honor.[cclxix]

      m1 Sarah
      m2 ---
      m3 Nancy Howard, (div)
      m4 ---
      m5 Flor de Maria Coto Ardon, 1961 May 06, Las Vegas, NV
      b. 1935, Costa Rica

Children (m3):

5.4006 i.   + Barbara Ann Ludlow

Children (m4):

5.4007 ii.   Arthur Ludlow   (ca. 1950-1967)
5.4008 iii.   William Ludlow   (ca. 1952-1980)

Children (m5):

5.4009 iv.   + John Henry Ludlow
5.4010 v.   + William deRushe Ludlow
5.4011 vi.   + Elizabeth Anne Ludlow

5.4006 Barbara Ann 6 Ludlow *(John5 Leo4 Albert3 Israel2 Israel1)*
　　　　b. 1946, FL

　　　　m. John Racich

5.4009 John Henry 6 Ludlow *(John5 Leo4 Albert3 Israel2 Israel1)*
　　　　b. 1963, CA

　　　　m. Carol Grassi, 1988, Huntington Beach, CA (div)
　　　　b. 1959, CA

　　　　(=) Rebecca Lynn Pilkington

Children(m1):

5.5010 i.   Alexandra Jayne Ludlow   b. 1989, CA
5.5011 ii.   Ryan Michael Ludlow   b. 1991, CA

Children(=):

5.5012 i. @ Rachel Leilani Ludlow   b. 2004, CA

5.4010 William de Rushe 6 Ludlow *(John5 Leo4 Albert3 Israel1)*
　　　　b. 1965, CA

5.4011 Elizabeth Anne 6 Ludlow *(John5 Leo4 Albert3 Israel2 Israel1)*
　　　　b. 1966, CA

5.2009 Frederick Hubert Israel "Fritz" 4 Ludlow *(Albert3 Israel2 Israel1)*
    b. 1886 Apr 06, Waukesha, WI
    d. 1963 Dec 13, Milwaukee, WI
    bur: Prairie Home Cemetery, Waukesha, WI (Section-G Block-62 Lot-1)

    m. Helen Beatrice Monaghan, 1920 Jan 19, Waukegan, IL
    b. 1895 May 01, Milwaukee, WI
    d. 1964 May 11, Milwaukee, WI
    bur: Prairie Home Cemetery, Waukesha, WI (Section-G Block-62 Lot-1)

Children:

5.3006 i.   + Margaret Laura Ludlow

5.3006 Margaret Laura 5 Ludlow *(Frederick4 Albert3 Israel2 Israel1)*
    b. 1920 Nov 01, Milwaukee, WI
    d. 2001 Oct 03, Milwaukee, WI
    bur: Prairie Home Cemetery, Waukesha, WI (Section-G Block-62 Lot-2)

Attended St. Joseph's Academy, St. Louis, MO; Milwaukee University School and Prospect Hall, Milwaukee, WI; graduated from the Foster School of Design, New York.

    m1 James V. Bahan, Jr., 1947 Nov 15, Milwaukee, WI[cclxx] (div.1950)
    b. 1919 Sep 07, Fairfield, CT
    d. 1999 Feb 14, Tom's River, NJ
    bur: unk

Son of James Vincent Bahan, Sr. and Anna (Byrnes).

    m2 Frank Hanke*
    b. 1911 Oct 02, Milwaukee, WI
    d. 2001 Oct 17, Milwaukee, WI
    bur: Prairie Home Cemetery, Waukesha, WI (Section-G Block-62 Lot-2)

    *Son of Roman and Anna Rutowski. Changed surname to Hanke.

Helen Adela Slacum Ludlow

From the collection of the Ludlow Heritage Museum

"Elmwood Hall"

Photo courtesy of Patrick Snadon.

Home of Israel L. Ludlow, purchased in 1831.

By the mid-1840's it was sold to brother-in-law George R. Kenner. The next owner was James Goodloe, who purchased the home in 1846. [cclxxi]

"The Historic Ludlow Homestead" [cclxxii]

Photo from the collection of the Ludlow Heritage Museum

The Last Four Survivors of the Crew of the USS Black Hawk,
Flagship of Admirals David D. Porter and Samuel P. Lee,
US Navy, Mississippi Squadron
Albert S. Ludlow is third from the left, the others are unidentified.

Photo from the collection of the Ludlow Heritage Museum

James Thompson Bryant &
Louise Ludlow Bryant Read

Photo courtesy of Sylvia Weller

Erich Volkmann, Sr. & Dorothy Read Volkmann
1917

Photo courtesy of Sylvia Weller

Somerset Hall, summer residence Of William Butler Kenner, Ludlow, Kentucky.

Elmwood Hall, summer residence of George R. Kenner, Ludlow, Kentucky,
and former residence of Israel L. Ludlow.

The Kenner Connection

After the death of Israel Ludlow, Charlotte Chambers Ludlow was married a second time, in 1808, to Rev. David Riske. Riske, a minister of the Associate Reformed Presbyterian Church, was originally from Ireland and had received his education in Edinburgh, Scotland. Rev. Riske had been sent to America to establish churches. He traveled throughout southwest Ohio, preaching and forming new congregations.

The couple set up residence at the Ludlow Mansion, and they became the parents of two daughters. Although not Ludlow descendants, these half-sisters to Charlotte's children by Israel Ludlow, would prove to be a very important and influential part of the Ludlow family. These two daughters, Ruhamah and Charlotte Riske, married two brothers from Louisiana, George Rappele Kenner and William Butler Kenner.

The Ludlows and Kenners shared common interests, one being the pride of owning and managing their large estates. Of course Israel owned "Elmwood", an estate of one thousand acres, and James owned the farm at Ludlow Station, but the Kenners, too, owned large properties. Butler's Louisiana plantation, "Oakland" was located along the Mississippi River above New Orleans. George was half-owner, with the youngest Kenner brother, Duncan, of the plantation "Ashland", also on the Mississippi but further upriver.[cclxxiii]

The Ludlows and Kenners also took great pride in their stables of horses. They raised Arabians and Thoroughbreds in their stables; hiring professional trainers and building race tracks on their estates. Another shared interest among some, if not all, of the menfolk seems to have been gambling, either at a race track or at various card games.[cclxxiv]

Although they lived in Louisiana most of the year, the Kenners maintained summer homes at "Elmwood" near half-brother Israel L. Ludlow. George Kenner purchased "Elmwood Hall" from Israel L. Ludlow for use as his summer residence, as the Ludlows moved into a nearby house which became known as the "Ludlow Homestead". Butler Kenner then purchased 32 acres of Elmwood land and constructed a summer home, "Somerset Hall", on his acreage.

Despite the common interests the Kenners and the Ludlows shared, cultural and philosophical differences, must have created some division between them, even if unspoken. How does one reconcile the abolitionist views of the Ludlows with one of the largest slaveholding families of the south?

Israel L. Ludlow was, indeed, a slave owner, as both his "Elmwood" and his "Caney Creek" properties were large properties requiring much labor to maintain. Yet, Ludlow's will, written in 1845, stipulated that his Texas slaves were to be freed after five years of servitude.[cclxxv]

However, George Kenner acquired the property and the slaves the following year, and when Kenner died in 1852, his brother Duncan took the slaves to Louisiana to work on his plantation at "Ashland".[cclxxvi]

Several sources reference the Kenner family and their slaves.

The youngest Kenner brother, Duncan, seems to have been a reasonable master to his slaves. One slave, Abe Hawkins, in the years following the Civil War, offered to provide monetary assistance to his former master, who had fallen into hard times. Duncan was also known to provide clothes and gifts for his slaves at Christmas. But operating a large plantation, Duncan was dependent on slave labor. It is known that Duncan was willing to give up slavery in order to preserve the Confederacy during the Civil War but, by that time, the end of the practice was imminent anyway.[cclxxvii]

Several sources provide insight into George Kenner and the subject of slavery. In January of 1846, George Kenner placed a notice in a northern Kentucky newspaper that two of his slaves, "Jim and William" had escaped, offering a reward of $400 for their return.[cclxxviii]

Another source, more compelling than the newspaper notice, is the testimony of a former slave named Alexander Kenner, who was interviewed in 1863.

"Mr. Kenner said he was born in Louisiana. His father was the Hon.George R. Kenner. His father had seven children by his mother, and then married a white woman, but told his mother she might go away. She went away, and took with her four of her children. Another was subsequently born. Mr. Kenner intended to make her free, but did not give her free papers. They went to St. Louis, and the mother worked for several years at washing, and he (Alexander) carried out the clothes. She throve exceedingly well. After seven years, Mr. George Kenner sold out the plantation , with all its rights, to his brother, Hon. Duncan F. Kenner, and his mother bought three of her children, including Alexander, for $1800....

The oldest brother had remained on the plantation, and became valuable to Mr. Kenner as a rider of his race horses, and he would not let him go."

The testimony then reveals this oldest brother's name as William.[cclxxix]

Could this be the same " William" referenced in the newspaper as an escaped slave, belonging to George Kenner? If so, William was not merely a slave George Kenner owned, but also his own son.[cclxxx]

Again, despite any differences that separated them, the Ludlows and the Kenners remained closely allied through the years and, to this day, the Kenner name is still used in the family, a sign of their significance within the family.

The Riske/ Kenner Families

Charlotte Chambers Ludlow
1768-1821
m2 Rev. David Riske, 1808
?-1818

Children(m2):

1)   Ruhamah Riske
2)   Charlotte Riske

1) Ruhamah Riske
b. 1811, "Ludlow Station", OH
d. 1885 Feb 24, Philadelphia, PA
bur: Green-wood Cemetery, Brooklyn, NY (Section-90 Lot-5655)

        m. William Butler Kenner, 1832 Sep 11, Cincinnati, OH
        b. 1810 Mar 11, LA
        d. 1853 Sep 24, LA
        bur: unk

        Children:

        Philip Minor Kenner
        Sarah Belle Kenner
        Josephine Kenner
        Charlotte Ludlow Kenner
        Mary Minor Kenner
        Frederick Butler Kenner

2) Charlotte Ludlow Riske
b. 1812, "Ludlow Station", OH
d. 1860 Sep
bur: Green-wood Cemetery, Brooklyn, NY (Section-181 Lot-12346)

        m1 George W. Jones, 1832 Oct 03

        m2 George Rappele Kenner, 1840 Mar 11
        b. 1812 Jan 18, New Orleans, LA
        d. 1852 Sep 25, Matagorda Co., TX
        bur: unk

        Children(m1):

        Emily Jones
        Georgine Jones

John Alfred Dumont Burrows Grave Marker
Spring Grove Cemetery
Section 106 Lot 2

A SPECIAL NOTE OF APPRECIATION

To my many collaborators over the years who have assisted with this genealogy ,
I acknowledge your assistance and thank you for your kindness.

Evelyn Auld
Ona Auld
Stuart Auld
Kenner Beecroft
Cathy Benedict
John David Benedict
Steve Benjamin
William Benjamin
Scott Breckinridge, Jr.
Shar Dahl
Mary Jane Dellenback
Charles Eipper
Eric Engle
Hugh Goodhue
Nick Goodhue
Elizabeth Graham
Margaret Ludlow Hanke
Bob Harris
Susan Henderson
Ken Herrick
Mary B. Hodge
William Hoyt
William "Jeff" Jeffery
Louise Kelly
Clara Longstreth
Edmund D, Ludlow
Flora Ludlow
Lydia Ludlow
John Ludlow
Louise Marsteller
Adele Mayer
Frederic McMahon
Archie Messenger
John Messenger
Judy Messenger
Franklin Hoyt Moore
Howard Palmer
Eden Pearson
Scott B. Peyton
Marty Riessen
Lydia Rivers

Dudley Robinson
Lisa Rost
Sally Stokes
Sam Stokes
Florence Stout
John Sweet
Martha Thomas
Anita Treants
Dorothy Turner
Kyle Wasielewski
Sylvia Weller

Historians, Librarians and Archivists

Anita Carlton, Galesburg, IL
Elizabeth Carlson, Paxton, IL
Florence Elliott, Paxton, IL
Rebecca Hosta, Cincinnati Art Museum
Andrea Matlack, Archivist, P.E. Church
Alicia Mauldin-Ware, USMA, West Point, NY
Martha McMunn, Pulaski Co., IL
Russell Meyer, Frontenac, MN
Dorothy Moore, Sewickley Historical Society
Jami Peele, Olin Library, Kenyon College
Mildred Ruth, West Palm Beach, FL
Barbara Scott, Saratoga Springs, NY
Kathleen Tatum, Matagorda Co., TX

Libraries and Societies

Allen County Public Library, Ft.Wayne, IN
Boston Public Library, Boston, MA
Cincinnati Historical Society, Cincinnati, OH
Clayton Genealogical Library, Houston, TX
Enoch Pratt Free Library, Baltimore, MD
King Library, UK, Lexington, KY
Kenton County Public Library, Covington, KY
LDS Family Library, Salt Lake City, UT
Lexington Public Library, Lexington, KY
Lloyd House, Alexandria , VA
Ludlow Heritage Museum, Ludlow, KY
National Archives, Washington, DC
Newberry Library, Chicago, IL
Olin Library, Kenyon College, Gambier, OH
Hamilton County Library, Cincinnati, OH
Sewickley Valley Historical Society, PA
Tulsa City-County Library, Tulsa, OK
University of Wisconsin, Stout, WI
Virginia State Library, Richmond, VA

Charles Gay, Slacum Family Historian
Frank Jansen, Friganza Family Historian
Patrick Snadon, Professor of Architecture, UC

The home of Edward H. Maxwell and Louisa (Ludlow) Maxwell.
27 River Road
Ludlow, Kentucky

Notes, Sources and Thoughts of Possible Interest

An Introduction to the Ludlow Family, p. 1

The book, _"Sketch of the Life and Times of Col. Israel Ludlow, One of the Original Proprietors of Cincinnati"_, (Henry Benton Teetor, Cincinnati: Cranston & Stowe, 1885), was published eighty years after Col. Ludlow's death. The poem "Fifty Years Ago: A Song of the Western Pioneers", was written by William D. Gallagher and then set to music by composer W. C. Peters. It was published in 1846, and bore the inscription "Respectfully Dedicated to the Descendants of Israel Ludlow, A Pioneer of 1788".

The Ancestry of Israel Ludlow, p. 3-4

[i] _Sources include:_
"A Genealogy of the Descendants of William Ludlam, of Southampton, L.I.", Julia Parish. Ludlam - N.S.. - 1896
"Ludlows in America in the 17th, 18th, and 19th Centuries: A Source Book from the Series Surnames in America about People Bearing the Name of Ludlow, Ludlam, and Ludlum, with Emphasis on Those Who Lived in New York and New Jersey". McKee, Ruth V., Minneapolis: Surname Sources, 1989. Print.
"William Ludlam of Southampton, Long Island", Mann, Conklin, _American Genealogist vol. 20, p. 2 (1943)_.
"Ludlow Family", by James B. Ludlow, dated 1938, a copy is in the collection of the Hamilton County Public Library, Cincinnati, OH,
[i] _"A Genealogical History of the Ludlow Family"_, Noah Miller Ludlow - Riverside Printing House – 1884.

Israel Ludlow, pp. 7-11

[iv] _Now Cumminsville/Northside area of Cincinnati._
[v] _Obit, [Cincinnati] Western Spy, January 24, 1804._
[vii] _now Maysville, Kentucky._
[viii] _Among these were Daniel Cooper (1773-1818), also from Long Hill, NJ, and a fellow surveyor; Stephen Burrows, whose son would marry into the Ludlow family; older half-brother John Ludlow and younger brother William Ludlow._
[ix] _Memoir of Charlotte Chambers"_, Lewis H. Garrard, Privately Printed, Philadelphia, 1856, p. 48.
[x] _Pickard, Bill. "Israel Ludlow: The Man That Surveyed Ohio." Ohio History Connection Archaeology Blog. Ohio History Connection, 10 Nov. 2009. Web. 02 Aug. 2015._
[xi] _ibid._
[xii] _Magazine of Western History. Vol. 11. Cleveland, Ohio: n.p., 1884. Print., p. 406._
[xiii] _A letter from Elnathan Kemper to William Kemper, February, 1804.,_
Kemper Family Papers and Correspondence, Cincinnati Historical Society, (MSS qK32 series 2 box 1 letter # 85.
[xiv] _Memoir of Charlotte Chambers"_, Lewis H. Garrard, Privately Printed, Philadelphia, 1856, p. 28.
[xv] _E.D. Mansfield....During this time, the Ludlow Mansion was rented out to Jared Mansfield. Mansfield had been appointed the Surveyor-General of the Northwest Territory to continue the surveying work in the region._
[xvi] _The marriage date was December 15, 1808, with Rev. Joshua Lacy Wilson officiating._
Caldwell, John Day. "Pioneer Marriage Records of Hamilton County, Ohio, 1791-1820." N.p., n.d. Web.
[xvii] _"Memoir of Charlotte Chambers"_,

James Chambers Ludlow, pp. 15-68

[xviii] *Now Cumminsville/Northside area of Cincinnati.*

[xix] *Obit, Cincinnati Daily Gazette, August 17, 1841.*

[xx] *"Biographical Annals of Franklin County, Pennsylvania", vol. 1, p.14.*

[xxi] *"An American Family: It's Ups and Downs Through Eight Generations from 1650 to 1880", Edward N. Clopper, Standard Printing and Publishing, Huntington, WV, 1950, p.103.*

[xxii] *"The 1836 Executive Committee members were James C. Ludlow, Rees E. Price, James G. Birney, Isaac Colby, William Donaldson, John Melendy, Gamaliel Bailey, Thomas Maylin and C. Donaldson." Ohio Anti-Slavery Society. "Proceedings of the Ohio Anti-Slavery Convention", Putnam: Beaumont and Wallace, 1835.*

[xxiii] *"An American Family: It's Ups and Downs Through Eight Generations from 1650 to 1880", Edward N. Clopper, Standard Printing and Publishing, Huntington, WV, 1950, p.340.*

[xxiv] *Obit, Cincinnati Daily Gazette, December 17, 1845.*

[xxv] *Obit, Cincinnati Daily Gazette, January 15, 1852.*

[xxvi] *Spring Grove Cemetery burial record.*

[xxvii] *Obit, New York Times, November 20, 1925.*

[xxviii] *"American Queen : The Rise and Fall of Kate Chase Sprague, Civil War Belle of the North and Gilded Age Woman of Scandal", by John Oller, 2014,Da Capo Press, A Member of the Perseus Books Group, Boston.*

[xxix] *Obit, New York Times, April 29, 1905.*

[xxx] *Obit, New York Times, October 22, 1956.*

[xxxi] *Marriage notice, New York Times, March 20, 1910.*

[xxxii] *Obit, New York Times, August 7, 1965*

[xxxiii] *"The New Amsterdam Singers", by Elizabeth Gariti.*

[xxxiv] *"Spindle and Bow" , Bevis Longstreth - Hali - 2005 , and "Return of the Shade".*

[xxxv] *"Weddings: Molly Rauch, Benjamin Longstreth", New York Times, July 2, 2000.*

[xxxvi] *Obit, New York Times November 2, 1965.*

[xxxvii] *Ibid.*

[xxxviii] *"Barbara Hoyt to be Bride of N. P. Stokes 2d", The Brooklyn Daily Eagle, January 23, 1940 p. 17.*

[xxxix] *Obit, "Isaac N. P. Stokes, 91, Lawyer During New Deal and U.N. Birth", New York Times, August 14, 1998.*

[xli] *Information provided by Sam Stokes.*

[xlii] *Email statement from Sally Sims Stokes, July 8, 2015.*

[xliii] *"Karuna Center for Peacebuilding." Karuna Center for Peacebuilding. N.p., n.d. Web. 04 Sept. 2015.*

[xliv] *"Karuna Center for Peacebuilding." Wikipedia. N.p., n.d. Web.*

[xlv] *"Sustaining the League of Women Voters in America", Cashin, Maria Hoyt. N.p.: n.p., n.d. Print.*

[xlvi] *Obit, New York Times, November 14, 1937.*

[xlvii] *Obit, "Taylor, Beatrix ("Trixie") Benjamin, New York Times, November 11, 2005.*

[xlviii] *Marriage notice, New York Times, Sep 18, 2005..*

[xlix] *Email, Steve Benjamin, August 18, 2015.*

[l] *Wikipedia, "Beatrix Hoyt".*

[li] *Obit, The Inter Ocean [Chicago], October 11, 1886, p. 5.*

[lii] *Obit, "Samuel Ludlow", The Bloomington, Illinois, Pantagraph, September 4, 1949.*

[liii] *Obit, "Harvey E. Thomas", Leelanau Enterprise, October 23, 2014.*

[liv] *email from Judy Messenger, Aug 11, 2015.*

[lv] *Ibid.*

[lvi] *Now, Andrew Charles Cully; he was adopted by David K. and Lynn B. Cully.*

[lvii] *Obit, Chicago Sun-Times, May 15, 1990.*

[lviii] *"Marty Riessen." Wikipedia. N.p., n.d. Web.*

[lix] *Obit, Indianapolis News, March 12, 1954.*

[lx] *Obit, Indianapolis News, March 25, 1954.*

[lxi] *Ralph Nader Congress Project. Citizens Look at Congress; John Dellenback, Republican Representative from Oregon.* Washington, D.C.: Grossman Publishers, 1972.

[lxii] Marriage notice, Madison [WI] Capital Times, June 30, 1951, p. 4.

[lxiii] "The Chicago Medical Recorder", Volume 24, The Medical Recorder Pub. Co., 1903, p. 383.

[lxiv] Obit, Chicago Tribune, March 8, 1931.

[lxv] World Biography. New York: Institute for Research in Biography, 1948. Print. P. 351.

[lxvi] Frederick Schipsky." Vancouver Symphony Orchestra. N.p., n.d. Web. 04 Sept. 2015.

[lxvii] Obit, Boston Globe, August 1, 2013.

[lxviii] Obit, "Edward Forester Jr. (1926-2014)", Chicago Tribune, August 8, 2014.

[lxix] Obit, Hibbing [MN] Daily Tribune, Dec, 19, 2012.

[lxx] Letter from Shar Dahl,

[lxxi] Letter from Shar Dahl,

[lxxii] renewed 2012, Aug 11, McGregor, MN.

[lxxiii] Marriage Notice, Cincinnati Daily Gazette, July 14, 1843

[lxxv] Secretary's Report: no. 11, Harvard College, Class of 1865, Geo. H. Ellis Company, 1921, pp. 9-10.

[lxxvi] Obit, "Marjorie E. Eipper", Springfield [OH] News-Sun, 20 Aug 2007.

[lxxvii] Obit, "Florence Louise (Eipper) Stout), Chicago Tribune, 4 Apr 2004.

[lxxviii] Obit, "Paul Richard Stout", Chicago Tribune, Jan 2, 2011.

[lxxix] Obit, Los Angeles Daily Times, January 12, 1898.

[lxxx] Obit, New York Times, April 26, 1936.

[lxxxi] Nevada State Journal, April 15, 1906. This was one of several national newspapers that reported the tragic crash of Israel Ludlow's "aeroplane".

[lxxxii] Obit, New York Times, May 4, 1908.

[lxxxiii] New York Marriage Records, 1686-1980", FHL microfilm 1558496

[lxxxiv] Canadian Birth Record, Ontario.

[lxxxv] Death of Mrs. Hunt", Cincinnati Enquirer, May 20, 1913 p. 8.

[lxxxvi] Marriage notice, Cincinnati Daily Gazette, July 19, 1854.

[lxxxvii] "Dictionary of Louisiana Biography", Louisiana Historical Association, New Orleans, 1988.

[lxxxviii] Obit, Cincinnati Daily Gazette, May 1, 1873.

[lxxxix] "Biographical Annals of Franklin County, Pennsylvania", Vol. 1.

Martha Catharine Ludlow, pp. 79-124

[xc] Obit, Lexington Observer & Recorder, October 27, 1834.

[xci] Family tradition asserted that the Ludlow daughters, Martha Catharine and Sarah Bella, were sent to Philadelphia for their education. However, considering that their husbands had ties to Lexington, Kentucky, it seems more likely that they were educated there, a cultural city considered then as the "Athens of the West".

[xcii] The 1829 Cincinnati City Directory lists the Dudley residence as "Front Street, between Vine & Race".

[xcii] Obit, Paxton [IL] Record, May 6, 1875.

[xcv] Obit, Lexington Herald, February 25, 1902.

[xcvi] Obit, Lexington Herald, September 21, 1911.

[xcvii] Obit, Lexington Herald, August 19, 1920.

[xcviii] Gates, Edwards. "Men of Mark in America: Ideals of American Life Told in Biographies of Eminent Living Americans ... With an Opening Chapter on American Ideals by E.E. Hale." Vol. 1, 2. Men of Mark Pub. Co.: Washington, 1905. Print. pp. 173-175.

[c] Obit, New York Times, October 21, 1941.

[ci] Susan Kneass Laursen, email, dated July 29, 2015.

[cii] "The Sharples-Sharpless Family", Anderson, Bart. West Chester, PA: n.p., 1966. Print.

ciii "Ralph Earle Hines." Ralph Hines, CPT, Marine Corps, Springfield MA, 19Feb67 15E062. N.p., n.d. Web. 03 Sept. 2015.

civ Obit, "Mary (Hines) Hodge", Philly.com, Jun 15, 2005.

cv Marriage notice, New York Times, May 6, 1934.

cvi Marriage notice, Bucks County Courier Times, March 8, 1973.

cvii Obit, Lexington Herald, July 28, 1914.

cviii Obit, Lexington Herald, March 21, 1957.

cix Obit, Lexington Herald, May 17, 1971.

cx Obit, Lexington Herald, May 25, 1955.

cxi "Miss Dudley Robinson Marries Mr. Neil Robinson", Charleston [WV] Daily Mail, Apr 20, 1936..

cxii Obit, "Mining Engineer, Firm Chief Dies", The Charleston [WV] Gazette, March 11, 1974.

cxiii "Caroline Robinson to be Married...", Charleston [WV] Gazette, October 29, 1970.

cxiv "Miss Margaret Maury Robinson Married to Robert Reishman", Charleston [WV] Gazette Mail, August 4, 1968.

cxv Obit, Lexington Herald, October 14, 1941.

cxvi Obit, Lexington Leader, May 12, 1904, p. 8, col. 3.

cxvii Obit, New York Times, December 26, 1964.

cxviii Obit, Lexington Herald, August 2, 1941.

cxix Kentucky Marriage Records, 1973-1999, Kentucky Department for Libraries and Archives, Frankfort, KY

cxx "ExploreUK." Scott D. Breckinridge, Jr. Collection, 1801-2000, 1980-2000 -. N.p., n.d. Web. 03 Sept. 2015.

cxxi "The CIA and the US Intelligence System", Breckinridge, Scott D. Boulder U.a.: Westview Pr., 1986. Print.

cxxii Wikipedia: "SS Maasdam"

cxxiii "John Stephens Graham." Wikipedia. Wikimedia Foundation, n.d. Web. 03 Sept. 2015.

cxxiv Obit, Lexington Herald, April 12, 1943.

cxxv Obit, "John Thomas Vance", Helena [MT] Independent Record, June 15, 2008.

cxxvi Obit, Baltimore Sun, February 1, 1960.

3.3013 For more info see "Varina Breckinridge of Temora", by Marion Majer Katz, Little Patuxent Review.

cxxvii Obit, Church Life [a newsletter of the Protestant Episcopal Church], June 1901.

cxxviii "Between Me and Thee", Cleveland, OH., Burrows Bros., 1888.

cxxix Marriage Notice. Cincinnati Daily Gazette, June 10, 1843.

cxxx Obit, Cincinnati Daily Gazette, August 30, 1850.

cxxxi The Burrows family, like the Ludlows, were from New Jersey prior to settling in Cincinnati.

cxxxii Marriage notice, Cincinnati Daily Gazette, December 2, 1858.

cxxxiii Obit, Church Life [a newsletter of the Protestant Episcopal Church], November 1899.

cxxxiv Obit, Cincinnati Daily Gazette, June 6, 1863.

cxxxv "Civil War Veteran is Called by Death", Berkeley Daily Gazette, June 18, 1924, p. 1.

cxxxvi Obit, San Francisco Examiner, August 11, 1959.

cxxxvii Obit, San Francisco Chronicle, November 6, 1956.

cxxxviii Email from Kennan Herrick, Jr.

cxxxix Ibid.

cxl Obit, Oakland Tribune, April 27, 2007.

cxli Obit, San Francisco Chronicle, July 17, 1931.

cxlii Obit, Berkeley Daily Gazette, July 16, 1931.

cxliii Marriage notice, Cincinnati Daily Gazette, July 11, 1866.

cxliv "The Purple and Gold", Chi Psi, Clinton, NY, 1883, p. 193.

cxlv Obit, "Harris, Mrs. Virginia Crawford", Charleston [WV] Gazette, Apr 25, 1954.

cxlvi Obit, Scottsdale Progress, March 14, 1977, p. 2.

cxlvii "The Colorado School of Mines Magazine", vols. 11-13, p. 119.

cxlviii Email, Bruce Crawford, dated August 13, 2015.

cxlix "Miss Easterday is Mr. Crawford's Bride", Charleston [WV] Daily Mail, Dec 24, 1933.

[cl] *Email, Bruce Crawford, dated August 13, 2015.*

[cli] *Marriage notice, "Miriam Alice Hall Weds Mr. Crawford", Charleston [WV] Daily Mail, July 12, 1960.*

[clii] *Marriage notice, "In Local Society", Charleston [WV] Gazette, May 22, 1930.*

[cliii] *Marriage notice, Cincinnati Daily Gazette, October 16, 1845.*

[cliv] *Obit, Cincinnati Commercial Tribune, August 24, 1909.*

[clv] *Obit, Covington [KY] Journal, October 9, 1852.*

[clvi] *Marriage notice, Cincinnati Daily Gazette, March 22, 1854.*

[clvii] *Obit, Covington [KY] Journal, December 15, 1851.*

[clviii] *Email from Kyle Wasielewski, August 12, 2015.*

[clix] *Ibid.*

[clx] *Now part of the Cumminsville/Northside area of Cincinnati.*

Sarah Bella Ludlow, pp. 129-142

[clxi] *"Obituary, Mrs. Justice John McLean", Cincinnati Enquirer, January 14, 1882, p. 4.*

[clxii] *"Personal Memories", E. D. Mansfield, R. Clarke & Co., Cincinnati, 1879.*

[clxiii] *Obituary, Mrs. Justice John McLean", Cincinnati Enquirer, January 14, 1882, p. 4.*

[clxiv] *Among these were John McDonogh, an advocate of liberating American slaves and expatriating them to Liberia; Gamaliel Bailey, whose papers are in the collection of Princeton University, and which includes correspondence from both John McLean and Sarah Bella McLean; and Edwin M. Stanton.*

[clxv] *Obit, Cincinnati Daily Gazette, January 28, 1837.*

[clxvi] *Ibid.*

[clxvii] *Marriage Notice, Cincinnati Daily Gazette, May 12, 1843.*

[clxvii] *Obit, Cincinnati Daily Gazette, April, 5, 1861.*

[clxix] *"As an associate justice, McLean authored 160 majority opinions and 30 dissents. He was one of the few justices who published his circuit opinions. McLean wrote a number of antislavery opinions, including one as an Ohio Supreme Court justice in Ohio v. Thomas D. Carneal (1817), limiting the ability of slaveholders to take slaves into free states. In 1848 he publicly stated that to exist, slavery needed positive law, and that consequently — unless authorized by Congress, slavery could not exist in a territory."("The Supreme Court of Ohio & The Ohio Judicial System." John McLean. N.p., n.d. Web. 22 Aug. 2015.)*
It was this same Thomas D. Carneal who built Elmwood Hall, home of Israel L. Ludlow.

[clxx] *Obit, Cincinnati Commercial Tribune, October 29, 1901..*

[clxxi] *"The Garrard Family in Frontenac", Frances Densmore,*

[clxxii] *Ibid.*

[clxxiii] *Obit, Washington Post, February 22, 1951.*

[clxxiv] *New York Passenger List, S.S. Minnehaha, Arrival at New York from London, England, September 8, 1913.*

[clxxv] *Letter from Kenner S. Beecroft, dated 1992 Jun 8.*

[clxxvi] *Email from Kenner Beecroft, dated 2015 July 27.*

[clxxvii] *ibid..*

[clxxviii] *Obit, "Capt. E. Chester Beck", Annapolis Capital, March 4, 1987, p. 8.*

[clxxix] *Information supplied by Stuart Beck, undated*

[clxxx] *Obit, Washington Post, December 28, 2012.*

[clxxxi] *"Frederic Garrard McMahon." (born October 5, 1927), American Executive, Investment Company Executive. N.p., n.d. Web. 18 Aug. 2015.*

[clxxxii] *Obit, Westchester NY newspapers, Dec 17, 1990..*

[clxxxiii] *"Kenner Garrard." Wikipedia. Wikimedia Foundation, n.d. Web. 03 Sept. 2015.*

[clxxxiv] *"Wah-to-yah and the Taos Trail", ...*

[clxxxv] *Marriage notice, Dunn County [WI] News, March 7, 1902.*

[clxxxvi] *"The Bartlett Tree and Thee", Hope Bartlett Taylor, c. 1996, Gateway Press, Baltimore, MD, p. 147.*

clxxxvii Obit, Dunn County [WI] News, June 15, 2005 p. A6.

clxxxviii Marriage notice, Dunn County [WI] News, June 8, 1906.

clxxxix Obit, Cincinnati Enquirer, December 17, 1915.

cxc Obit, "Taps for Jeptha Garrard: Civil War Hero Expires at Queen City Club", The Cincinnati Enquirer, December 17, 1915, p. 16.

Israel L. Ludlow, pp. 149-170

cxci now Ludlow, Kentucky.

cxcii Obit, Cincinnati Daily Gazette, April 23, 1846.

cxciii Transcribed notes copied from the "Old Family Bible, in possession of Samuel Ludlow, Paxton, Ill. This book was purchased "anno domini 1802 by Israel Ludlow".

cxciv A letter dated March 18, 1822, addressed to Secretary of War, John C. Calhoun... "Sir, I am informed that the name of Israel Ludlow is under consideration for an appointment as a cadet in the Military Academy.
This young gentleman, with whom my personal acquaintance is very slight, is (I believe) the posthumous son of Col. Israel Ludlow, formerly of Cincinnati, one of the earliest settlers in that part of the country; and much respected by a numerous acquaintance. His mother, also highly respected, while she lived, died last year, leaving the young gentleman now 18 years of age an orphan and in circumstances , as I understand, that make the appointment desirable and which his friends are desirous he should obtain. I have understood that the patrimony is reduced by the support and education of a large family, so as to leave him hopes of but a slender inheritance—his character is [illegible]as I have heard; or had an opportunity to know.
I am, sir, with much respect, your ob[edient] servant, Ethan A. Brown"

Letter from Israel L. Ludlow, dated April 7th, 1822, to Secretary of War, John C. Calhoun... "Sir I have this day received a letter from Mr. E. A. Brown enclosing a cadets warrant [sic] stating the time when I must appear at West Point and the qualifications necessary as one of the members of that institution. And I will with pleasure attend at the place and time specified in the warrant [sic] and shall endeavour by diligent study and punctual observance to the instructions given to obtain a favourable repourt[sic].
Your Obediant [sic] Servt, Israel L. Ludlow"

cxcv Israel L. Ludlow's records at West Point include multiple notations of "absent from Reveille"; "bed not strapped"; "absent from church"; "conduct unbecoming a cadet"; "sleeping in study hours", and other infractions. The list, including dates for each offense, is recorded for the period of July-December, 1822.

cxcvi For research into Israel L. Ludlow's time at West Point, I am indebted to Alicia Mauldin-Ware, Archives Curator, Special Collections and Archives Division, at the United States Military Academy.

cxcvii 1829 Cincinnati City Directory, Israel is listed at the boarding house of Mrs. Sarah Benbridge.

cxcviii The only road into the estate was along the river's edge from Covington, a route often flooded or muddy or otherwise impassable. To solve the problem of transportation for Elmwood, and for Northern Kentucky in general, Israel Ludlow worked on several projects. One was the planning of Burlington & Dry Creek Turnpike, which was to connect Covington to Burlington in Boone County, Kentucky, through Elmwood and its western neighbor, Bromley. A second project was a proposed railroad route from Cincinnati to cities in the south, to attract business from southern markets. Israel Ludlow was appointed to represent the City of Cincinnati at a meeting in Knoxville, Tennessee, for the planning of the project. A third project involved Israel Ludlow on a committee to plan a bridge to be built spanning the Ohio River to connect Cincinnati to its southern neighbor, Covington. The collapse of the American economy in 1837 delayed all three projects until years later. Construction on the turnpike did not begin until around 1850; the railroad appeared in the 1870's as the Cincinnati Southern Railroad. As for the bridge project, it too was delayed until the end of the Civil War, at which time it was built and still stands today as the Roebling Suspension Bridge between Cincinnati and Covington.

^{cxcix} "*An American Family: It's Ups and Downs Through Eight Generations from 1650 to 1880*", Edward N. Clopper, Standard Printing and Publishing, Huntington, WV, 1950, p. 259.

^{cc} "Whereas, on the 7th day of January, 1839, a judgment was obtained in the superior court of the county of Hamilton, in favor of the state of Ohio, and against Israel L. Ludlow, David T. Disney and Joseph Graham, for the sum of ten hundred and seventy-two dollars and sixty cents, for using and giving certain arms belonging to the state of Ohio, and deposited in the city of Cincinnati, to volunteer companies who embarked from said city, to assist the Texians in their late struggle for independence..." *Journal of the House of Representatives of the State of Ohio*, vol. 37, The State, 1838, p. 561.

^{cci} Matagorda County, Texas, Deed Records, Ludlow/Wightman transaction dated May 2, 1842, Deed Book E, pp. 454-457. Also deed dated May 2, 1842, Book E, p. 461, "grantor, Israel Ludlow and grantee, Ira R. Lewis, "1/2 of negro slaves & cattle, etc."

^{ccii} Samuel Patterson was at the "raising of a large building at Washington [TX], that there was a shower of rain which made the timber slippery and that a large log or plate had suddenly slipped down, the end of which caught him and injured him so much he died the next day!"

["*An American Family: It's Ups and Downs Through Eight Generations from 1650 to 1880*", Edward N. Clopper, Standard Printing and Publishing, Huntington, WV, 1950. P. 330].

Likewise, the death of Elias Wightman was sudden and unexpected, as well. The agreement between Ludlow and Wightman exchanged the Texas property of Wightman for Ludlow's "Elmwood" estate. At Wightman's arrival in northern Kentucky, he was taken suddenly ill and died. His widow contested the agreement between her husband and Ludlow, which resulted in a monetary settlement for her, and Ludlow retaining ownership of both properties. ["Notice---Ludlow Mortgage on Lands in Texas". Licking Valley Register, April 2, 1842, p. 3]

^{cciii} Will of Israel L. Ludlow, Will Book 1, pp. 46-49, Independence, KY.

A transcribed copy, with notes by Walter T. Ritchie, attorney, also notes a particular sentence within the document, which reads... "In all cases when I speak of my children I mean such as are or may be born to me of my dear wife". Ritchie made a note in the margin, "The inference seems to be that testator had others".

Just a few years after the burial of Israel L. Ludlow at Spring Grove another burial took place in the family lot. In September of 1852, Randolph J. Stone, a young visitor from New Orleans, died at Cincinnati's Gibson Hotel of "bilious fever". One month after his burial in Section 41 in Spring Grove, the remains were reinterred in the Ludlow family lot in an unmarked grave. What was his relationship to the Ludlow family that he was buried with them? Is it possible that he was buried elsewhere originally to avoid any possible connections to the Ludlow family? So far, no answers.

^{cciv} Obit, Cincinnati Daily Gazette, April 23, 1846, p. 2. Note: He was 41, not 40; and instead of the Presbyterian burying ground he was buried at Spring Grove.

^{ccv} Much of the easternmost portion of the estate was sold or auctioned, and later became incorporated as the town of West Covington in 1856. The remainder was known as "Elmwood" until 1864, when it was incorporated as the city of Ludlow, KY.

^{ccvi} Her father was a sea merchant; the first mayor of Alexandria, Virginia and a close associate of George Washington. Her brother, George Washington Slacum, served as the US Consul to Brazil and was a boyhood friend of Robert E. Lee. Another brother, William Slacum, was appointed by President Andrew Jackson in 1835 to visit the Oregon Territory and gather information about the region. His report, read to Congress in 1837, advocated American control of the region. For more information about the Slacums, see: Benham, Mary Louisa Slacum, and Elizabeth Jane Betsy. Stark. "*Recollections of Old Alexandria and Other Memories of Mary Louisa Slacum Benham*" (1802-1884). Place of Publication Not Identified: Publisher Not Identified, 1977. Print.

^{ccvii} Obit, Cincinnati Commercial, March 7, 1872.

^{ccviii} It was said that the river view reminded her of her home in Alexandria, Virginia, on the banks of the Potomac River. Elmwood Hall had been built ten years earlier by Thomas D. Carneal, whose family had originally also been from Alexandria, and like the Slacums, had attended Christ Church.

For more detailed information about Elmwood Hall, including floor plans, see

Lancaster, Clay. "*Antebellum Architecture of Kentucky*" Lexington, KY: U of Kentucky, 1991. Print.

[ccix] See the Walter Ritchie papers, Cincinnati Historical Society.

[ccx] "A Romance of Morgan's Rough Riders: The Raid, the Capture and the Escape", The Century Illustrated Monthly Magazine, Volume 19; Volume 41, p. 420.

[ccxi] Worcester Ludlow was born in January of 1846 and only lived until October of that year, succumbing to tuberculosis like his father. He was most likely named after Dr. Noah Worcester, a prominent Cincinnati doctor who served as the family physician for several Ludlow family members. Dr. Worcester, who specialized in the treatment of tuberculosis, was well-respected in the community and much loved by his patients. He also contracted the disease and died in 1847.

[ccxii] "An Interesting History: Death of a Woman Who Was Five Times Married", Cincinnati Enquirer, May 3, 1885, p. 13.

[ccxiii] Ibid.

[ccxiv] 1850 Kenton County, Kentucky, census.

[ccxv] Louisa "instituted proceedings for divorce. One day William started for Maysville by boat, and disappeared, being reported drowned. Good Mrs. Ludlow, the mother of Louisa, said it looked much like one of William's tricks to stave off the divorce, and so the suit was pressed to a successful issue. Later on the old lady's prediction was verified, as William was heard from: but he never returned."

("An Interesting History: Death of a Woman Who Was Five Times Married", Cincinnati Enquirer, May 3, 1885, p. 13)

[ccxvi] No further reference to William Barnet Phillips has been located after his marriage to Louisa. It is unknown at this time if the marriage ended in divorce or by his death.

[ccxvii] "Spur Up Your Pegasus: Family Letters of Salmon, Kate and Nettie Chase", edited by James P. McLure, Peg A. Lamphier, and Erika M. Kreger, 2009, The Kent State University Press, Kent, Ohio.

[ccxviii] The area previously known as Elmwood had been incorporated as the town of Ludlow, Kentucky, in 1864.

[ccxix] Among any other problems in their marriage, Edward and Louisa Westcott were trying to cope with Georgia's unpredictable and difficult behavior, which included running away from home. As a result, for a time, Georgia was committed to an asylum.

[ccxx] Edward and Louisa Maxwell are listed in the 1880 census in Worcester, Massachusetts. Interestingly, Mr. Maxwell, whose occupation was given as a liquor merchant in records previous to his marriage to Louisa, listed his occupation in the 1880 census, after his marriage to Louisa, as "millionaire".

Accusations were made by Louisa's former husband, Westcott, that Edward Maxwell was exercising "undue influence over his wife, whose intellect is destroyed or greatly impaired by the excessive use of stimulants" and that his reason for divorcing her was her "gross intemperance". ("An Answer is An Answer", Cincinnati Enquirer December 18, 1876, p. 7.

[ccxxi] Even after Louisa Ludlow Maxwell's death, her family was back in court when her daughter, Georgia, contested her mother's will.

[ccxxii] His full name is believed to be William Henry Harrison Goodloe. His father, James Tompkins Goodloe, owned a large foundry and cotton mill in Cincinnati. He purchased Elmwood Hall from George Kenner in 1846. When James Goodloe later sold Elmwood, he moved to Mound City, Illinois, building a foundry there. During the Civil War, the foundry was seized by the U.S. government for use as a military hospital, and Goodloe was never compensated for his financial loss. After his death, his widow sought compensation from the government, but no record has been located regarding any final judgment on the matter.

[ccxxiii] William Goodloe, "wounded at Churubusco and was reported to have died of his wounds in several documents and historical accounts of the war. In fact, however, he survived. Resigning from the service at the end of 1847, he appears to have collected a disability pension until his death, sometime after 1877."

("StrategyPage.com - Combat Information Center Analysis, Facts and Figures about Military Conflicts and Leaders." StrategyPage.com - Combat Information Center Analysis, Facts and Figures about Military Conflicts and Leaders. N.p., n.d. Web. 01 Sept. 2015.)

[ccxxiv] "Commanding Officers at Newport Barracks, 1803-1894",

[ccxxv] Marriage notice, Cincinnati Daily Gazette, October 7, 1854.

[ccxxvi] Obit, Richmond [VA] Dispatch, October 9, 1861.

[ccxxvii] William Mitchell, Jr., lf Richmond, Virginia, was a wealthy and well-known silversmith.

[ccxxviii] "The History of the College of William and Mary", Applewood Books, 2010 p. 140, (Class of 1846-57).

[ccxxix] "Bookkeeper at Walker's factory, the home address was listed as Second Street between Main and Cary", Richmond [VA] Directory, 1858-59, p. 143.).

A portrait of William Hubbard Mitchell III is in the collection of the Museum of the Confederacy, Richmond, VA.

[ccxxx] "Virginia, Marriages, 1785-1940," database, FamilySearch (https://familysearch.org/ark:/61903/1:1:XR6K-H39 : accessed 30 July 2015), Wm Barnet Phillips and Louise Mitchell, 07 Nov 1861; citing Richmond, Henrico, Virginia, reference p 24 # 20; FHL microfilm 31,855.

[ccxxxi] Trinity Episcopal Church marriage records, Covington, KY.

[ccxxxii] Obit, Richmond [VA] Dispatch, October 9, 1861.

[ccxxxiii] "The Bryant Divorce Case", Cincinnati Enquirer, June 21, 1894, p. 6.

[ccxxxiv] Obit, Boston Times, February 11, 1918.

[ccxxxv] Obit, New York Times, September 22, 1949.

[ccxxxvi] Obit, New York Times, October 17, 1933.

[ccxxxvii] "Four Brilliant Years", The Publisher's Weekly, January 13th, 1934, Vol. CXXV, no. 2. I am indebted to author Romy Wylie for providing a copy of this article.

[ccxxxviii] Marriage notice, New York Times, June 9, 1925.

[ccxxxix] Obit., Bangor Daily News, January 11, 1997.

[ccxl] According to her burial record at Spring Grove Cemetery, Georgia's full name is listed as "Georgia Ludlow McAnrow Connor", and her late residence is listed as "4056 Lake Park Av, Chicago, Ill". Although the address in Chicago was listed to a John A. McAnrow, no marriage, census or other record has been found to explain the "McAnrow" connection. An Illinois death record for her has not yet been found.

[ccxli] "Georgia Conner Succeeds in Breaking Her Mother's Will", Cincinnati Enquirer, June 3, 1887, p. 4.

[ccxlii] "A Reclaimed Daughter... ", Cincinnati Enquirer, May 22, 1887, p. 12.

[ccxliii] George Howard Ludlow, seems to have had ongoing health concerns, possibly as a result of some childhood illness. By early 1852, he was not well, and doctors suggested a milder climate may be of some benefit, so he left for Texas. Family friend and nephew of Salmon P. Chase, James Ralston Skinner, persuaded Adela to leave Cincinnati, too, so she took William and Albert with her north to Buffalo, where she spent the summer with the Skinner family there. At the beginning of August, Adela received word that George Howard's condition had worsened and that he had left Texas for Cincinnati. Ralston convinced Adela to have him travel to Buffalo. George Howard made the journey to Cleveland, and from there boarded the steamer "Crescent City" for the last part of his journey, but died on board the ship before its arrival at Buffalo. His burial record of Spring Grove Cemetery lists his cause of death as "disease of the heart". Ralston Skinner felt "implicated" in the death of George Howard Ludlow, and in later years he suffered "mental illness", associated with this event. See "Spur Up Your Pegasus" p.131.

[ccxliv] Obit, "W.S. Ludlow Dies; Ohio History Expert; Last Surviving Grandson of the Founder of Cincinnati... ", New York Times, Aug 1, 1931.

[ccxlv] Prentice's wife, Henrietta, was a step-daughter to Helen Adela Ludlow's sister, Maria Slacum Benham. The family stayed with the Prentice family while Israel L. Ludlow was in Texas. According to the Louisville city directory of 1841, the Prentice home was located on Main Street, between Walnut and Chestnut Streets.

[ccxlvi] Obit, Cincinnati Enquirer, July 31, 1931.

[ccxlvii] "The Alumni and Former Student Catalogue of Miami University: Including Members of the Board of Trustees and Faculty, 1809-1892". Oxford, OH: Press of the Oxford News, 1892. Print.

[ccxlviii] The lease, which was for a period of 99 years, expired in 2001, at which time the Southern Railroad exercised their option to purchase the 86 acre tract for $100,000 from the Ludlow heirs.

[ccxlix] The 1904 Cincinnati City Directory lists William Ludlow as president of the Lagoon Company, with his office address as 1008 Commercial Tribune Building. His home address was given as "flat 10, 339 Sycamore".

[ccl] "Capitalist: Is Shot by Gunmen... "' Cincinnati Enquirer, February 18, 1919, p. 14.

[ccli] Obit, New York Times, October 6, 1919.

[cdii] *She was the daughter of Romeo Friganza, a superintendant of the navy yard at Mound City, Illinois, during the Civil War. Sarah Friganza Ludlow's niece, born Delia O'Callaghan, became the star of stage and screen known as Trixie Friganza.*

[cdiii] *"Ludlow Base Ball Club", Ludlow Reporter, April 17, 1875, p. 3.*

[cdiv] *There seems to have been several reasons for his relocation to Wisconsin. First of all, there was an attempted robbery reported at the homestead in December of 1874, one of an increasing number of cases of vandalism and violence in the town of Ludlow at the time. ["Attempted Robbery", Ludlow Reporter, December 25, 1874, p. 2] Secondly, Albert was indeed suffering from health issues, such as a "dormant ulcer" and kidney concerns. [Ludlow Reporter, Jan 30, 1875, p. 2, also Ludlow Reporter, February 13, 1875, p. 2].It was during this time that he and Sarah were going through marital difficulties and this may have been the primary cause for the move. It was at this time that they separated.*

[cdv] *"An answer and cross-petition was filed yesterday by the wife in the divorce suit of Albert Ludlow against Sallie Ludlow. The lady denies the husband's faithfulness alleged in the petition, and denies that she ever abandoned him, or his home, or their children. She says that he suggested to her in September, 1875 [should be 1874], to visit New York while he made a trip elsewhere to recruit his health; that she obeyed, he giving her the money to go; that upon her return he met her in Cincinnati, and told her he would not live with her any longer; that she was taken to a boarding-house over there, and that he has given her no money except $6 a week to pay her board, and that he has sent one of their children to California [Adela], and will not permit her to live with the other one."*
("Divorce Literature", Cincinnati Enquirer, April 28, 1877, p. 7)

[cdvi] *"The Ludlow Pictures", Inter Ocean (Chicago), December 24, 1884, p. 12.*

[cdvii] *Albert Ludlow's art collection included works such as "Saint Helena and the Emperor Constantine Presented to the Holy Trinity by the Virgin Mary", by Corrado Giaquinto. This work is currently in the collection of the St. Louis Art Museum.*

Other works of art owned by Albert Ludlow included "St. Anne Ministering to Mary", attributed to Luis de Vargas; 'St. Anthony Healing the Lepers" by an unknown artist; "The Death of St. Joseph", attributed to Sebastian Ricci; "Christ Disputing with the Doctors", attributed to Raphael; "Hagar and Ishmael", by an unknown artist, "portrait of the French statesman, Jean Baptiste Colbert, painted from life by Pierre Mignard" (Inter Ocean (Chicago), January 20, 1895, p. 23.) and many, many others.

Many of Albert's artworks were placed on loan to several museums. For example, "The Annual Report of the Cincinnati Museum Association" (Cincinnati: Robert Clark & Co., 1882) p. 47, lists such works as "Landscape", by C. Poellemberg; "Landscape" by Hobbema; two "Landscapes" by Jacob More and a German Village Scene, "Halt of the Hussars" by A. Eckert, on loan from Albert Ludlow. The two Jacob More landscapes mentioned were still in the possession of the Cincinnati Art Museum many years later, after the death of Albert. The loan cards stored in the museum records confirm that both paintings "were destroyed at the request of his estate", but no explanation is provided as to why.

Albert also had several artworks destroyed in Chicago's Calumet Club fire of January, 1893.

At least one painting was, possibly, a work by Rubens. See "Art Collector's Mystery", Chicago Tribune, February 9, 1971, Section 2, p. 4.

Other artworks owned by the family included large individual oil paintings of Helen Adela Slacum; Maria Slacum Benham; George Washington Slacum; and William Augustus Slacum. A pastel portrait of George Howard Ludlow by an unknown artist was also in the collection.

[cdviii] *New York Tribune, June 11, 1888, p. 2..*

[cdix] *After Albert's death, William donated land in the city of Ludlow for use as the "Albert S. Ludlow Memorial Park".*

[cdx] *"Divorce Literature", Cincinnati Enquirer, April 28, 1877, p.7*

[cdxi] *Obit, Kentucky Post, February 13, 1897.*

[cdxii] *Marriage notice, Waukesha Freeman, October 7, 1896.*

[cdxiii] *Obit, Cincinnati Times-Star, January 6, 1913.*

[cdxiv] *Obit, Tulsa Daily World, March 4, 1941.*

[cdxv] *ibid.*

[cclxvi] *Waukesha Freeman*, May 17, 1917.

[cclxvii] *"Tulsan Downs Axis Bomber Without Firing A Shot"*, Tulsa Daily World, March 21, 1943.

[cclxviii] *"Ludlow-Bahan Nuptials"*, Milwaukee Sentinel, November 16, 1947.

[cclxix] The purchase date of September 8th, 1846, is provided by the case *"C. Kenner v. Jas. Goodloe"* (*"Reports of Cases Argued and Adjudged in the Superior Court of Cincinnati in 1854-1855"*, Cincinnati: O. R. Clarke & Co., 1877)at which time James Goodloe acquired Elmwood Hall plus twelve acres of land, for the amount of sixteen thousand dollars. Elmwood Hall is located at 244 Forest Avenue in Ludlow, Kentucky.

[cclxx] This was the site of the Ludlow residence at the time of General John Hunt Morgan's escape in November of 1863. The Ludlow Homestead was destroyed by fire in 1913. (Kentucky Post, July 15, 1913. p. 5)

The Kenner Connection pp. 175-177

[cclxxi] Although "Oakland" was destroyed by flooding many years ago, "Ashland" still stands today as a neglected ruin of its former glory, now owned by Shell Oil Co.
The mansion has been used in several movies, including "Band of Angels" (1957); "The Beguiled" (1971); "The Autobiography of Miss Jane Pittman" (1971), and "The Long, Hot Summer" (1985). "
Wikipedia contributors. "Ashland Plantation." Wikipedia, The Free Encyclopedia, 29 May. 2015. Web. 4 Aug. 2015.

[cclxxii] *"Forest Hill was Won in a Card Game"*, Kentucky Post, December 25, 1900, p. 5. Since written more than fifty years after the death of Israel L. Ludlow, the article is not trustworthy, but it does indicate that Ludlow had a reputation of being a card player and gambler.

[cclxxiii] The Ludlow and Kenner men took great pride in the ownership and management of their large estates. This pride also included their livestock, especially their horses. Duncan Kenner's stables included such horses of fame as Grey Fanny, Medoc, Kendall, Panic, Pat Golray, Luda, Rupee and Louis d'Or. Duncan had artist Edward Troye create portraits of his horses. (*"A Leader Among Peers ; the Life and tTmes of Duncan Farrar Kenner"*, Craig Bauer, Lafayette, Louisiana: Center for Louisiana Studies, University of Southwestern Louisiana, 1993.) George and Duncan Kenner had a racetrack at their Ashland plantation. Likewise, a racetrack was also located on the Elmwood estate, as well, and James and Israel L. Ludlow also owned horses of note, including Caravan, Alexander, and Kitty Fisher. (*"The Western Agriculturist, and Practical Farmer's Guide."*, Cincinnati: Robinson and Fairbank, 1830.) (The Thoroughbred Record, v. 87-88, Lexington, KY.,p. 280)

[cclxxiv] By that time, he lived at the Ludlow Homestead, having sold the Elmwood Hall property to George Kenner.

[cclxxv] Salmon P. Chase was also concerned with the plight of the Texas slaves who were to be have been freed by Israel L. Ludlow's will. When Adela Ludlow visited the Chase family in January of 1848, Chase asked Belle to speak to Adela about the Texas slaves. See *"Spur Up Your Pegasus"*.

[cclxxvi] Duncan F. Kenner was appointed by Jefferson Davis to seek military and financial support from European countries during the Civil War. In exchange for their support, the Confederacy would end the practice of slavery. Kenner's mission failed to achieve the desired results and shortly thereafter the war ended. (*"A Man of Pleasure, and a Man of Business: the European Travel Diaries of Duncan Farrar Kenner, 1833-1834"*, Duncan Farrar Kenner - Garner Ranney - Center for Louisiana Studies — 1991)

[cclxxvii] *Licking Valley Register*, January 31, 1846, p. 2.

[cclxxviii] *"Slave Testimony: Two Centuries of Letters, Speeches, Interviews, and Autobiographies"*, John W. Blassingame - Louisiana State University Press - 1977, pp. 392-393.

<u>Format, Symbols & Abbreviations Used in the Genealogy</u>

Individual Number; Name; <u>Line of Descent</u>

b. birth: year, month, day; location

d. death: year, month, day, location

bur: burial location   c. Cremated   unk: unknown or not provided

m. marriage, year, month, day, location   (=) relationship other than marriage   (div.) divorce

@ adopted, step-child or other   + additional information

Mark and Yolanda
at the Ludlow Heritage Museum
Photo by Jim Callaway

I can sum it all up in just four words, I am...**not related...just fascinated.**

Yolanda and I married in 1986, and we bought a house in her hometown of Ludlow, Kentucky. I had never had a town to call home before but, since then, this little riverside community has become my hometown, too.

In those early days, Yolanda told me what she knew of our town's humble beginnings...and of its founding family, the Ludlows. Intrigued to learn more, we went libraries and cemeteries; searched courthouse files and church records. Eventually, Yolanda and were flying to Boston and Los Angeles; to Milwaukee and Houston, and to other points in between, and before we realized it...the fascination had become an obsession!

Over the years we've met many of the family, while corresponding with others via letter, phone or email. It has been an interesting journey, and we've made friends along the way. Yolanda and I will always appreciate the experiences and memories we have collected as a result of our quest.
The time has now come to find a project to occupy our next thirty years!

Finally, remember that a lasting legacy has nothing to do with passing on wealth, fame or possessions. The real legacy is living life to the fullest in service to others, sharing love and laughter and taking pride in your family, your heritage and yourself.
This will be remembered as your true legacy.

Mark

193

Name Index